Contents

Test-taking TIPS

General

- Count the number of pages to make sure that there are no missing pages.

- Read the instructions carefully so that you know what to do and how to do it.

- In multiple-choice questions, read all the four options before deciding which is the correct answer.

- Write neatly.

- Always check your answers and writing after you have completed the test.

READING

- Read the text once before reading the questions.

- When reading a question, find out what is being asked.

- Look for clue words.

- Look for the information in the text based on the clue words.

- In multiple-choice questions, look for consistent grammar between the stem (the part with a blank for completion) and the response (the choice to be put into the blank to complete the stem). If it does not sound right, it is probably wrong.

- If you see "use information from the text and your own ideas", it means that you can use specific details from the reading selection and at the same time include your prior knowledge and experience of the topic in your answer.

WRITING

- Read the instruction carefully so that you know exactly what you are asked to write about.

- Pay attention to the key words such as "describe" and "explain".

- "Describe" means that you have to use words to tell the reader how something looks and feels. It is like using words to create a mental picture for the reader.

- "Explain" means you have to use words to make clear how something works or why something happens or works the way it does. You need to give supporting details step-by-step.

- Ask yourself the five "W-" and one "H-" questions to generate ideas for your writing. These question words are: who, what, when, why, where, and how.

- Jot down the ideas that come to your mind. Organize them and write a draft.

- Arrange the ideas in the order which you would like to present them.

- Organize your writing in paragraphs: the introductory paragraph, the body paragraph(s), and the concluding paragraph.

- Each paragraph should preferaby begin with a topic sentence, followed by supporting details or examples. End the paragraph with a concluding sentence or a sentence that leads to the next paragraph.

- After writing, check your spelling, grammar, and punctuation.

Bears

How many types of bears do you know? Some well recognized types   1
are the polar bear, black bear, brown bear, and honey bear.

Polar bears live in the Arctic. They eat marine animals and birds.   2
Polar bears are covered in thick white fur so that they can hide in
the snow. They also have a layer of insulating fat to help them survive
the extreme cold. Not only are polar bears the greatest hunters of
all the bears, they can also swim 100 kilometres without stopping to
rest!

The black bear weighs about 136 kilograms, which is about as heavy   3
as two adults. It averages 1.8 metres long, the height of a tall man.
Like all bears that live in cold climates, the black bear hibernates
throughout winter.

Brown bears can be found in Europe, Asia, and North America. One   4
of the best known types of brown bears is the grizzly bear, which can
weigh as much as 450 kilograms. Grizzlies also hibernate throughout
winter.

The largest of all the bears is a type of brown bear called the Kodiak   5
bear. At 2.75 metres tall, it weighs as much as 725 kilograms –
almost as much as eight people combined. Kodiaks eat plants and
roots, but they love fish too, especially salmon. Every year, large
groups of Kodiaks gather in streams to catch salmon as they swim
their way upstream to the spawning grounds.

Honey bears live in Southeast Asia and are only about 1.2 metres   6
long and weigh 45 kilograms. In fact, they are the smallest of all
bear species.

The headline in the *Toronto Star* on August 27, 2005 was bad news   7
for bears. It read, "Fish Bad for Grizzlies". If bears eat fish rather
than berries and plants, they would have a high level of pollutants in
their bodies because the fish are swimming in polluted waters. When
they get contaminated, they pass the pollutants on to the bears.

Maybe one day you will have a job as a naturalist. It might be your   8
responsibility then to track and count bear populations, record the
changes to their habitats, and suggest ways of protecting them.

Bear Attack

Bears are more curious than aggressive. They may approach, but will usually run if they sense that you are aware of their presence. Should you be confronted by a bear, there are ways to protect yourself. If it is going to attack, keep a cool head. The worst thing you can do is panic and run. Never try to outrun a bear because it moves much faster than you think. An average bear can run up to 40 kilometres an hour!

If the bear looks like it is going into a full confrontation, drop to the ground, roll into a fetal position, and cover your head, chest, and abdomen by rolling yourself into a tight ball. Usually, if you allow the bear to roll on you while you are still in a tight ball, the bear will give up and deem you dead. It will wander away.

1 In Canada, we do not find

    a   polar bears.

    b   honey bears.

    c   grizzly bears.

    d   Kodiak bears.

2 Read the following sentence from "Bear Attack" in the box.

It will wander away.

What does the word "wander" mean?

    a   walk casually

    b   walk cautiously

    c   sneak

    d   move disappointingly

3 Why is "Bear Attack" put in a box on page 5?

    a   It is unrelated to the article.

    b   It is the most important part of the article.

    c   The author thinks that it is some additional information that the reader may be interested in.

    d   The author wants to highlight the danger of bears.

4 Which of the following statements is true?

    a   Grizzlies like eating berries and fish.

    b   All kinds of bears hibernate in winter.

    c   The polar bear is the largest among bears.

    d   Honey bears are found in the warmer regions of North America.

5   Which of the following statements is NOT true?

     a   Salmon swim their way upstream to the spawning grounds.

     b   When fish get contaminated, they pass the pollutants on to the bears that eat them.

     c   The honey bear is usually shorter than a man.

     d   Polar bears have a layer of fat to help them store food.

6   Which of the following actions is wrong when you are confronted by a bear?

     a   Run as fast as you can.

     b   Drop to the ground.

     c   Curl up in a tight ball.

     d   Pretend that you are dead.

7   What is the theme of paragraph 7?

     a   The *Toronto Star* reported some bad news about bears.

     b   Bears would absorb pollutants after feeding on contaminated salmon.

     c   It is better for bears to eat berries and plants.

     d   There is a high level of pollutants in salmon.

8   What is probably NOT the job of a naturalist?

     a   Record the number of bears in a certain area.

     b   Make sure that bears do not eat contaminated salmon.

     c   See how bears' habitats change.

     d   Find ways to protect bears.

Roberta Bondar:
the First Canadian Female Astronaut

Roberta Bondar fulfilled a life-long dream. She became the first   1
Canadian female astronaut to go into space in 1992. This
accomplishment was the result of years of perseverance and
preparation. From the time that Yuir Gagarin circled the Earth in a
spaceship when Roberta was 16, Roberta was determined to be part
of the space program.

From an early age, Roberta had been fascinated with outer space.   2
She won numerous science fair competitions in high school, and
distinguished herself as a top student. She obtained a bachelor of
science degree, and went on to obtain three more degrees in
pathology, neurobiology, and medicine. By the age of 36, she had
completed her education and training and had also become a pilot.
She became an assistant professor of medicine at McMaster University
in Hamilton, Ontario.

Then one day, Roberta heard a radio announcement stating that 3
Canada was embarking on a space program – anyone interested in
becoming an astronaut was invited to apply. Roberta wasted no
time and filed her application immediately. More than 4000
applications were sent in, but only six were chosen. Roberta was
among them. She was sent to the NASA training facility to learn to
fly American spacecraft.

In 1984, a Canadian was chosen to be part of an astronaut team, but 4
the candidate was Marc Garneau, and not Roberta Bondar. In fact,
it was not until eight years later that Roberta got her chance to fly in
space. From January 22 to 30, 1992, Dr. Bondar flew on Space
Shuttle Discovery. During the mission, Roberta's duties included
analyzing and examining fellow astronauts for backbone strain and
stretching. She continued this work after her duty as an astronaut.

In 1998, Roberta was named to the Canadian Medical Hall of Fame 5
for her groundbreaking research in space medicine. She has received
the Order of Canada, numerous honorary university degrees, and
countless awards of recognition from various institutions and
associations. Roberta Bondar is truly a remarkable person who
achieved her dream.

Roberta has these words of encouragement for young people: 6
"Throughout your lifetime, you're always learning, growing, and
evolving. The reality is that you don't need to go into space to see
the world differently."

Space Shuttle Discovery

Discovery is one of three spacecraft in the Space Shuttle fleet belonging to the U.S. National
Aeronautics and Space Administration (NASA), along with Atlantis and Endeavour. First flown
in 1984, Discovery is the oldest shuttle in service.

Discovery was the shuttle that launched the Hubble Space Telescope. The second and third
Hubble service missions were also conducted by Discovery. It also carried Project Mercury
astronaut John Glenn, who was 77 at the time, back into space on October 29, 1998, making
him the oldest human being to venture into space.

1 Read the following sentence from paragraph 1 of the text.

This accomplishment was the result of years of perseverance and preparation.

What does "this accomplishment" mean?

a   being the first Canadian astronaut to be trained at the NASA

b   being the first astronaut

c   being the first Canadian astronaut

d   being the first female astronaut from Canada

2 What is the theme of paragraph 3?

a   The radio announcement was the best thing that had happened to Roberta.

b   Roberta was among the six chosen for the space program.

c   Canada was embarking on a space program.

d   Roberta joined the space program at the NASA.

3 Read the following sentence from paragraph 3 of the text.

Roberta was among them.

To whom does the word "them" refer?

a   the 4000 applications

b   the astronauts at the NASA

c   the female candidates

d   the six selected candidates

4 Read the following sentence from the text.

In 1998, Roberta was named to the Canadian Medical Hall of Fame for her groundbreaking research in space medicine.

Which of the following words is similar in meaning to the word "groundbreaking"?

a   significant

b   advanced

c   thorough

d   dramatic

5 Which of the following statements is NOT true?

a   Roberta became a pilot when she was 36.

b   Marc Garneau was a member of an astronaut team in 1984.

c   Both Marc Garneau and Roberta are Canadian.

d   Roberta started training as an astronaut in 1992.

6 Read the following sentence.

It also carried Project Mercury astronaut John Glenn, who was 77 at the time, back into space on October 29, 1998, making him the oldest human being to venture into space.

The sentence indicates that John Glenn has

a   travelled on Discovery before.

b   been trained with Roberta before.

c   travelled in space before.

d   been chosen for the mission because of his age.

Writing –
Humankind's Greatest Invention

Writing is fun, but it can also be a serious endeavour. Writing can be art or science. Writing is a great way to communicate information and feelings. Writing can inform and entertain. It can incite. It can reassure. It can change people's lives. It can change the world. And it is something we can all do. Writing is humankind's greatest invention.

1

Evidence of man's earliest attempt to communicate by "writing" things down can be found in caves. Yes, even cavemen wanted to make note of their activities; their 30 000-year-old hunting journals have been found on the walls in caves near Avignon, France.

2

Egyptian civilization also had their own form of picture art/communication, called hieroglyphs. The ancient Assyrians (in what is now northern Iraq) had a system called cuneiform. The Chinese pictographic system of writing began as early as 1500 BCE. Over time, all of these pictographic systems incorporated phonetic elements as well. The Korean and Japanese "alphabets", developed later, are phonetic in nature, although today, Japan also incorporates the Chinese system of writing into its language. Other Asian languages, such as Thai, are also phonetic in nature, meaning that the written symbols are based on sounds, not pictures or ideas.

3

The western alphabet was first developed in the Middle East, by the Phoenicians, in the area that is now Lebanon and Greece, hence the term "phonetic". With this phonetic system, we need only a small number of symbols, which can be combined in an unlimited number of ways, to write all the words we need. It is generally agreed that pictograph-based languages, such as Chinese, are harder to master, but not impossible. For example, while there are about 130 000 Chinese characters in existence, the average Chinese person needs to know only about 2000 to be able to read the newspaper.

4

From cave-wall art to the printing press and the World Wide Web, the expression of ideas through writing – and the dissemination of these ideas – has become accessible to so many people. Through blogs, for example, we can know what people are thinking and feeling about things on the other side of the world! We are truly living in a global village.

5

Ts'ang Chieh – the Inventor of Chinese Characters

Ts'ang Chieh was credited for inventing Chinese characters. His invention of the Chinese script was actually inspired by the footprints of birds and animals. He noticed that the lines and shapes were perceptible and distinct. Ts'ang Chieh then drew pictures of the objects according to their shapes and forms. In time, these pictures were reduced and simplified to a few lines and highly stylized, and became the early form of Chinese writing.

1 Which of the following is an example to illustrate that writing can reassure?

   a   an article about global warming

   b   a letter of encouragement from the principal

   c   a list of things to do

   d   a recipe

2 The Japanese alphabet

   a   is phonetic-based.

   b   originated from the Chinese pictographic system of writing.

   c   incorporated phonetic elements.

   d   is different from other Asian languages because it is pictograph-based.

3 Egyptian hieroglyphs

   a   were discovered in caves near Avignon.

   b   originated in northern Iraq.

   c   shared the same root as cuneiform.

   d   were pictograph-based.

4 Which of the following statements is true?

   a   The Phoenicians were credited for inventing the western alphabet.

   b   Chinese has a small number of phonetic symbols that can be combined to form an unlimited number of words.

   c   Lebanon and Greece shared the same pictograph-based writing system.

   d   An average Chinese newspaper uses about 2000 characters.

5 Read the following sentence from the text.

From cave-wall art to the printing press and the World Wide Web, the expression of ideas through writing – and the dissemination of these ideas – has become accessible to so many people.

What does the word "dissemination" mean?

a distribution

b sharing

c use

d confirmation

6 What is the theme of paragraph 5 of the text?

a The World Wide Web has helped extend the reach of ideas through writing.

b Blogs have become a popular form of sharing ideas through writing.

c Cave-wall art can now be shared worldwide, thanks to the World Wide Web.

d It is easy for people to share ideas through writing in a global village.

7 What is the theme of "Ts'ang Chieh – the Inventor of Chinese Characters" in the box?

a Chinese characters were invented by Ts'ang Chieh.

b Ts'ang Chieh invented the first Chinese characters by following the footprints of birds and animals.

c Inspired by the footprints of birds and animals, Ts'ang Chieh developed the early form of Chinese characters.

d The Chinese script was based on distinct lines and shapes of birds and animals.

Urbanization

Do you know what "urban sprawl" is? Urban sprawl happens when 1
cities and towns expand, pushing more and more buildings and roads
into the countryside. Urbanization is a part of our world, and people
lament the fact that we cannot enjoy the pleasures of nature as easily
as we were once able to.

Nowadays, many people in Canada are leaving their farms and their 2
homes in the countryside because Canada has become one of the
most urbanized countries in the world. It has become very difficult
to make a living outside cities.

Ethelwyn Wetherald was a well-known Canadian poet and journalist 3
born in Rockwood, Ontario in 1857. Much of what she wrote was
about nature and family life. She loved the natural world and
understood, even in her day, that there was an unhealthy side to
progress. Imagine what she would think if she were alive today.

Children in the City

by Ethelwyn Wetherald (1857 – 1940)

Thousands of childish ears, rough chidden,
Never a sweet bird-note have heard;
Deep in the leafy woodland hidden
Dies, unlistened to, many a bird.
For small soiled hands in the sordid city
Blossoms open and die unbreathed;
For feet unwashed by the tears of pity
Streams around meadows of green are wreathed.

Warm, unrevelled in, still they wander;
Summer breezes out in the fields;
Scarcely noticed, the green months squander
All the wealth that the summer yields.
Ah, the pain of it! Ah, the pity!
Opulent stretch the country skies
Over solitudes, while in the city
Starving for beauty are childish eyes.

Wetherald's Best Poems

In the autumn of 1907, a collection of Ethelwyn Wetherald's best poems was published, entitled, *The Last Robin: Lyrics and Sonnets.* It was warmly welcomed by reviewers and lovers of poetry. Earl Grey, then Governor-General of Canada, was so impressed by Wetherald's works that he wrote a personal letter of appreciation to her, and purchased 25 copies of the first edition for distribution among his friends.

1 Why does the author use quotation marks for "urban sprawl"?

    a   The author finds the term difficult to understand.

    b   The author wants to draw the reader's attention to the term.

    c   The author wants to highlight a new term.

    d   The term is used in an unusual way in the text.

2 Read the following sentence from the text.

Urbanization is a part of our world, and people lament the fact that we cannot enjoy the pleasures of nature as easily as we were once able to.

What does the word "lament" mean?

    a   feel sad about

    b   feel discouraged with

    c   accept

    d   deny

3 Ethelwyn Wetherald felt that

    a   Rockwood was too urbanized.

    b   nature had to give way to urban development.

    c   progress might not be all desirable.

    d   nature and family life would be destroyed by urbanization.

4 Which of the following statements about *The Last Robin: Lyrics and Sonnets* is NOT true?

    a   Earl Grey reviewed the collection and recommended it to his friends.

    b   The collection was published in 1907.

    c   Earl Grey complimented Wetherald for her impressive works.

    d   Earl Grey was the Governor-General in 1907.

5 According to the poem, "unlistened to" in line 4 of the first stanza of *Children in the City* refers to

    a   children in the city.

    b   children in the countryside.

    c   birds in the woods.

    d   birds in the city.

6 Read the following line from *Children in the City*.

For small soiled hands in the sordid city

What does the word "sordid" mean?

    a   unpleasant

    b   crowded

    c   polluted

    d   indifferent

7 Read the following line from *Children in the City*.

Scarcely noticed, the green months squander

"The green months" means

    a   the time for sowing.

    b   the time when vegetation starts to grow.

    c   the time to go green.

    d   the time to enjoy nature.

Cells: Our Genetic Makeup

The human body is made up of trillions of cells which come in over 200 types. Cells are too small to be seen by the human eye and must be viewed under a microscope. Cells are living organisms that eat food for energy and build body matter. The combination of cells forms other organisms in our body. There are particular cells that combine to construct bones, muscles, and skin. These groups of cells are supported by nerve cells that form our brain. Cells are responsible for the way we look, the things we are able to do, and for protecting us against germs. All living things – plants and animals – are made up of cells.

1

A cell is made up of fats, sugars, proteins, and nucleic acids such as DNA. When we eat, we feed the cells in our body. Food is taken in and broken down in our stomach and intestines. The blood carries these smaller particles of food to our cells.

2

The Father of Genetics

Gregor Mendel (1822-1884) was the first person to suggest the existence of genes. In the 1860s, Mendel studied inheritance in pea plants and hypothesized a factor that conveys traits from parent to offspring. He spent over ten years on one experiment. Although he did not use the term "gene", he explained his results in terms of inherited characteristics.

Our cells then take out the nutrients they require to build themselves and other new cells.

DNA consists of minute strings of genes lined up in each cell in a ladder-like pattern. The genes are what make proteins which are the building blocks for cells and the determiners of the various activities of the cells. Genes are what make human beings, as a species, look similar; they are also what give human beings their distinct features and talents.

3

Cells are covered by a membrane, but inside there are different organs. The nucleus, in the middle of the cell, stores the packages of genes called chromosomes. There are 46 chromosomes in 23 pairs in each nucleus of each cell in our body. The chromosomes come in pairs because they represent the combined contribution of the father and the mother from whom we get our characteristics. Have you ever had someone tell you how much you look like one of your parents? Height, weight, colour of hair, eyes, voice, and physical expressions are some of the commonalities you may possess as a result of your gene pool.

4

A Tricky Question

How many cells are there in a human being?

Some sources claim that the average adult human body is made up of 50 trillion cells, while others put the figure closer to 10 trillion. Yet some others state that there are approximately 100 trillion cells in the human body. All of these figures are just estimates, as there is yet a way to find out the exact number of cells in a human body. Also, the number will vary from person to person, depending on their size. To complicate matters further, the number of cells in your body is constantly changing, as cells die or are destroyed and new ones are formed. So even the number of cells in your own body is not static.

5

1 Which of the following statements is true?

a   DNA and genes look similar.

b   Voice is a characteristic passed on by parents.

c   Cells line up in the body in a ladder-like pattern.

d   Nucleic acids carry food particles to our cells.

2 Which of the following statements does NOT describe genes?

a   Genes determine a person's distinct features.

b   Genes are lined up in a ladder-like pattern.

c   Genes are covered by a membrane.

d   Genes determine the various activities of the cells.

3 In the middle of a cell are chromosomes that

a   store the nutrients for the cell.

b   come in 23 pairs.

c   determine how many cells a person has.

d   do not exceed 46 pairs.

4 The author includes information about Gregor Mendel in the box on page 20 most likely to

a   make the text more readable.

b   let the reader learn who discovered genes.

c   highlight the importance of Gregor Mendel.

d   let the reader know that this is not related to the text.

5 What was Gregor Mendel's ten-year long experiment about?

    a   to study the effects of inherited characteristics on pea plants

    b   to study the effects of inherited characteristics on human beings

    c   to find out if it is true that children inherit characteristics from their parents

    d   to consider the factors that affect the growth of pea plants

6 Why isn't there an agreed average number of cells in the adult human body?

    a   There are too many sources that do the calculations.

    b   Scientists are not able to agree which is the best way to find it out.

    c   There are far too many cells to count.

    d   The number of cells varies from person to person, and keeps changing even within one person.

7 Explain how cells, DNA, and genes are related to one another. Use information from the text to support your answer.

_____

_____

_____

_____

_____

The Great Pyramid of Ancient Egypt

The construction of the Great Pyramid has been a mystery to man   1
for centuries. How did the builders shape and transport over
2 300 000 stones without iron tools and transportation? How did
they move these massive blocks that weighed several tons each?
Why did they go to so much trouble?

In attempting to answer the questions, it is important to understand   2
how the Egyptians related to the world around them. The Egyptians
observed the phenomenon of nature. They believed in the balance
of all things. Sunrise gave way to sunset and nature revolved in
repetitive cycles. They were staunch believers in gods. The gods
controlled nature and therefore controlled their lives. Egyptians
believed in life after death. Similar to the cycles of nature, they
believed that they too followed a cycle: birth, life, death, and afterlife.
They believed that at death their bodies were transported to a place
they called the Land of the Dead where a person could carry on with
the rest of his or her existence. To facilitate this transition, they
buried their dead with a variety of household tools and items of
importance that would make things easier in the afterlife.

Egyptians believed that pharaohs were direct descendants of the gods 3
and were responsible for the order in their lives. Upon their death,
pharaohs would enjoy life forever with the gods. It was believed that
the pharaohs would cruise the skies watching over their people.
Therefore, the pharaohs were even more important to the people
after they died.

In approximately 2500 BCE, Pharaoh Khufu ascended to the throne 4
and declared himself to be the manifestation of both the gods, Horus
and Ra. A claim like this had never been made before and the
Egyptians were overwhelmed. They declared that Pharaoh Khufu
was the greatest pharaoh of all time.

Pharaoh Khufu lived up to this billing. He was a highly efficient and 5
organized pharaoh who travelled extensively throughout the
kingdom, particularly along River Nile, performing ceremonies to
honour the gods. He appointed governors to oversee each of the
districts, collect taxes, and administer the laws.

Pharaoh Khufu lived luxuriously, sparing no expense in entertaining 6
important guests and spoiling them with lavish gifts of gold, precious
jewels, and silks. Khufu knew that the wonderfully pleasurable life
he was leading would not last forever and that he must prepare for
the afterlife with the gods. So he started planning the construction
of the greatest pyramid of all time.

Construction of such a pyramid was a monumental task. There were 7
more than 35 000 labourers working full-time in a village-like setting
devoted to this project. Even without precise measuring tools, they
were able to shape the stones to identical specification with a variance
of less than eight inches between the shortest and longest sides of
the stones.

Pharaoh Khufu died in 2528 BCE at the age of 23. He was mummified, 8
a process lasting 65 days, and lowered into the sarcophagus inside
the pyramid.

1 Read the following sentences from the text.

The Egyptians observed the phenomenon of nature. They believed in the balance of all things.

Which of the following shows a balance of things?

a   afterlife

b   day and night

c   pharaohs and gods

d   pharaohs and pyramids

2 What is the theme of paragraph 6?

a   Khufu knew that he would die young and so he planned to build the greatest pyramid of all time.

b   Khufu wanted to prepare for his afterlife by constructing the greatest pyramid of all time.

c   Khufu wanted to build the greatest pyramid of all time to share with the gods.

d   Khufu wanted to build the greatest pyramid to store his wealth for use in his afterlife.

3 Ancient Egyptians believed that their pharaohs

a   would enjoy their afterlife in pyramids.

b   would become gods after death.

c   would still watch over them after death.

d   would rule the Land of the Dead after death.

4 Which of the following statements is true?

    a   Pharaoh Khufu's parents were Horus and Ra.

    b   It took more than 35 000 labourers 65 days to build Pharaoh Khufu's pyramid.

    c   The pharaohs controlled the phenomenon of nature.

    d   Ancient Egyptians believed that life followed a cycle.

5 Which of the following statements is NOT true?

    a   Ancient Egyptians believed that their pharaohs were gods' descendants.

    b   Pharaoh Khufu governed his kingdom efficiently.

    c   Pharaohs would go to the Land of the Dead after death.

    d   Pharaoh Khufu declared that he represented all gods.

6 What kind of pharaoh was Khufu? Use information from the text and your own ideas to support your answer.

_____

_____

_____

_____

_____

_____

Pauline Johnson:
the Mohawk Poet

Pauline Johnson (1861 – 1913) was born on the Six Nations Iroquois Reserve, near Brantford, Ontario. Her mother was an Englishwoman and her father a Mohawk chief. Her Aboriginal name was Tekahionwake.   1

Pauline toured Canada, the United States, and England giving dramatic readings of her poetry. She appeared on stage in a buckskin dress, a dress made of deer hide. She also wore a beaded belt that showed the beautifully intricate work of native designs. Her poems are beautiful and she gained an international reputation. She was very proud of her native ancestry and her poems reflect her love of nature.   2

In "The Pilot of the Plains", Pauline demonstrates her use of rich language and her ability to create pictures with words. The poem is a story of a native girl and a white man who are married but separated. The young wife is waiting in the village for her husband's return.   3

"Till the autumn came and vanished, till the season of the rains,
Till the western world lay fettered in midwinter's crystal chains,
Still she listened for his coming,
Still she watched the distant plains."

4

Do you see the changing seasons and the image of a cold winter's day? Try to imagine yourself as one of the hunters, or as the maiden, when reading this final stanza:

5

"Late at night, say Indian hunters, when the starlight clouds or wanes,
Far away they see a maiden, misty as the autumn rains,
Guiding with her lamp of moonlight
Hunters lost upon the plains."

6

The Indian maid is a ghost who has become "pilot of the plains". She has abandoned the warmth of her home to go into the winter night to look for her lost love, and is now a restless ghost guiding others to safety.

7

Pauline Johnson was proud of her Native heritage and wrote that "My aim, my joy, my pride is to sing the glories of my own people." Her life, career, and travels show that she was a woman who dared to do unexpected things and who was proud of where she came from. In her own time she was, as Mohawk writer Beth Brant says, a revolutionary.

8

Legends of Vancouver

In 1911 Pauline Johnson was dying of cancer. In an effort to pay for her medical bills and living costs, a group of Pauline's friends created a Trust Fund in her name and decided to raise money by publishing 15 of her *Legends of the Capilano* in what they called *Legends of Vancouver*. It was a tremendous success. *Legends of Vancouver* has become a classic of Canadian children's and native literature.

When Pauline Johnson died on 7 March, 1913, she was buried in Stanley Park, Vancouver among her beloved "Cathedral Trees". Later a cairn was erected over her grave and dedicated to the "memory of one whose life and writings were an uplift and a blessing to our nation".

1 Read the following sentence from the text.

In her own time she was, as Mohawk writer Beth Brant says, a revolutionary.

Which of the following shows that Pauline Johnson was a revolutionary?

a   She demonstrated the use of rich language.

b   She dared to do unexpected things.

c   She created pictures with words.

d   She appeared on stage in a buckskin dress.

2 Which of the following statements is true?

a   *Legends of Vancouver* was published in honour of Pauline Johnson.

b   Pauline Johnson published *Legends of Vancouver* and made it a success.

c   *Legends of Vancouver* was published to help raise money for Pauline Johnson.

d   *Legends of Vancouver* was later retitled to *Legends of the Capilano*.

3 Which of the following statements is true?

a   Pauline Johnson was noted for writing children's books.

b   Pauline Johnson's poems were mostly about lives on the Six Nations Iroquois Reserve.

c   "The Pilot of the Plains" is about a young wife waiting for her husband's return.

d   Pauline toured Canada, the United States, and England to perform dramas.

4 In "The Pilot of the Plains", the word "pilot" refers to

a   a Mohawk chief.

b   a brave Mohawk hunter.

c   an Englishwoman.

d   the ghost of an Indian maid.

5 Which of the following is an example to show that Pauline Johnson was proud of her Native heritage?

a   She appeared on stage in a buckskin dress.

b   Her poems reflect her love of nature.

c   Her Aboriginal name was Tekahionwake.

d   She toured Canada, the United States, and England.

6 Explain how Pauline Johnson used words to create the mysterious atmosphere in "The Pilot of the Plains". Use information from the text and your own ideas to support your answer.

_____

_____

_____

_____

_____

_____

Prince Edward Island's Sweetheart

Lucy Maud Montgomery, best known as the author of several   1
successful children's books, was born at Clifton, Prince Edward Island
in 1874. Like the heroine of her *Anne of Green Gables* series, Lucy
lost her own mother at the tender age of two. When her father
remarried, she, like Anne, was sent to live with aging people – in her
case, her grandmother and grandfather.

It is thought that much of Lucy's creativity, so clearly evident in her   2
writing, sprang from her early childhood imaginings about fairies
and other worlds. It was to such a world that Lucy could retreat to
escape the strict and emotionally repressive upbringing she received
from her grandparents.

As a teenager, Lucy wrote several poems and stories which were   3
published in her native Prince Edward Island. She became a
schoolteacher, but continued to write. It was not until 1908 that the

first book in her series about the red-haired, freckled orphan was published. This was followed in 1909 by the second book in the series.

In 1911, Lucy was married and left Prince Edward Island to move to Norval, Ontario and continued to write, making it her career. Although she wrote and published over 20 children's books and several adult books, it is for her stories about Anne of Green Gables that she became popular and famous, and continues to be so today.   4

Who can resist the story of the red-haired orphan, full of life and an active imagination, who comes to live with the elderly couple who thought they were adopting a boy to help them with the farm work? Anne's antics gave girls the freedom to escape from the confinements of being "young ladies" to consider doing things that had always been part of the male domain.   5

Anne of Green Gables has been translated into 15 different languages and put on film. The homestead of Lucy Maud Montgomery has become a Mecca to Anne enthusiasts from all over the world. Thousands of visitors flock to Prince Edward Island every year to visit her homestead, catch a glimpse of the Anne of their imaginations, watch plays, and enjoy the scenery that is so vivid in Montgomery's books.   6

Green Gables House

Green Gables is the name of a 19th century farm located in Cavendish, Prince Edward Island. The farm was owned by the Macneill family who were cousins of Lucy Maud Montgomery.

Montgomery visited the farm as a young girl and based her *Anne of Green Gables* series of books on the farm. She drew romantic inspiration from the house, as well as the surrounding area, including the "Haunted Woods", "Lovers Lane", and "Balsam Hollow".

Montgomery's novels turned Green Gables into a popular tourist destination beginning in the early 20th century. This led to the establishment of Prince Edward Island National Park in the 1930s. The park's boundaries encompassed the Green Gables homestead. Each year hundreds of thousands of visitors from around the world visit the site.

8

1 Read the following sentence from the text.

It was to such a world that Lucy could retreat to escape the strict and emotionally repressive upbringing she received from her grandparents.

What does the word "repressive" mean?

a   burdened

b   restricted

c   hurt

d   tormented

2 Read the following sentence from the text.

Anne's antics gave girls the freedom to escape from the confinements of being "young ladies" to consider doing things that had always been part of the male domain.

Which of the following was probably considered to be part of the male domain at Anne of Green Gables's time?

a   riding on horseback

b   playing in the backyard

c   doing chores on the farm

d   going to church

3 What is the theme of paragraph 6?

a   *Anne of Green Gables* is read all over the world.

b   *Anne of Green Gables* has made Montgomery's homestead a popular tourist spot.

c   Montgomery's homestead was vividly depicted in *Anne of Green Gables*.

d   *Anne of Green Gables* and Montgomery have made Prince Edward Island a top spot for tourists from all over the world.

4 Read the following sentence from the text.

The homestead of Lucy Maud Montgomery has become a Mecca to Anne enthusiasts from all over the world.

What does the word "Mecca" mean?

a   must-visit place

b   holy place

c   comforting place

d   dream place

5 "Lovers Lane" was

a   a street that led to Green Gables House.

b   a place where Montgomery met her husband.

c   part of Green Gables House complex.

d   a place in *Anne of Green Gables*.

6 Explain in what way Anne of Green Gables reflected the early life of Montgomery. Use information from the text and your own ideas to support your answer.

_____

_____

_____

_____

_____

_____

The Klondike Gold Rush

The Yukon Territory in the northern part of Canada   1
was the site of the largest gold rush ever. It attracted
more than 100 000 people over several years. The
gold rush all began when George Carmack, a gold
prospector, and his brothers-in-law found gold in
a creek near River Klondike on August 16, 1896.
The creek was renamed "Bonanza" to reflect the
size of the find.

When 80 miners on two ships left nearby Alaska   2
in the summer of 1897, news of the gold strike
travelled with them. Then, when the first ship
arrived in San Francisco, filled with bags and bags
of gold, it caused a sensation and people started
leaving their jobs and rushed to the Klondike in
search of gold! Eager to get there as soon as
possible, they booked passage on steamers, even
though they did not arrive in Alaska until the
following summer. Most of those who attempted

the trip to the Klondike on land, across the White Pass Trail, had to turn back when the winter came, but about 22 000 of them managed to make it through.

In the summer of 1898, Dawson, a small town in the Yukon, became the largest Canadian community west of Winnipeg. It had saloons, dance halls, and gambling parlours, but the rush ended as quickly as it had begun. By the end of 1899, Dawson's population had dwindled to a few miners. Everyone had left to follow the gold rush to Alaska.

3

What happened to George Carmack and his brothers-in-law, the original prospectors that first found gold in the Yukon? One remained a prospector, another ran a hotel in the Yukon, and George invested in real estate and a California mine. He died in Vancouver in 1922.

4

If you read about the Klondike Gold Rush in an American text, you will find that it has a very different story. The gold rush is seen as an Alaskan one, rather than having been started in Canada.

5

What Price Gold?

Many people who joined the gold rush died, or lost enthusiasm and either stopped where they were or turned back along the way. The trip was long, arduous, and cold. The people had to walk most of the way, using either pack animals or sleds to carry loads of supplies. The Northwest Mounted Police in Canada required that all those who go to the Klondike bring a year's worth of supplies with them. Even so, starvation and malnutrition were serious problems along the trail. The story of people having to boil their boots to drink the broth was widely reported, and may well have been true. Cold was another serious problem along the trail, as winter temperatures in the mountains of northern British Columbia and the Yukon were normally -20 degrees Celsius.

9

1 News about the gold strike in the Klondike

    a   was brought to the States by gold prospectors.

    b   spread to San Francisco.

    c   was released by newspapers in Alaska.

    d   generated interest across Canada.

2 Which of the following statements is true?

    a   George Carmack discovered a goldmine in Dawson.

    b   Two ships carrying 80 miners arrived in Alaska in 1897.

    c   The White Pass Trail led to the Klondike.

    d   There were about 22 000 people looking for gold in the Klondike.

3 Which of the following statements is NOT true?

    a   Bonanza Creek was near River Klondike.

    b   There were people in San Francisco who gave up their jobs for the Klondike Gold Rush.

    c   Carmack and his in-laws were the first to discover gold near River Klondike.

    d   The Klondike Gold Rush lasted a summer.

4 Read the following sentence from the text.

The creek was renamed "Bonanza" to reflect the size of the find.

What does the word "Bonanza" mean?

    a   sudden increase in wealth

    b   untapped treasure

    c   huge amount of gold waiting to be discovered

    d   hidden gem

5 In American articles about the Klondike Gold Rush,

a   the gold rush started in Alaska.

b   the gold rush originated in San Francisco.

c   Canada had nothing to do with the gold rush.

d   only Americans were involved in the gold rush.

6 The text under the topic "What Price Gold?" in the box is to illustrate

a   the hardship of the people working in the goldmines.

b   the difficulties people faced trying to join the gold rush.

c   the harsh winter climate of northern Canada.

d   the shortage of food in the Klondike because of the sudden increase in population.

7 Explain why the Northwest Mounted Police required all those who went to the Klondike to bring along a year's worth of supplies. Use information from the text and your own ideas to support your answer.

_____

_____

_____

_____

_____

A Christmas Tree for Boston

Every year since 1971, Nova Scotia has given an evergreen tree as a special Christmas gift to the people of Boston. The tree arrives in November, and stands in Boston Common, the city's prime location, through the winter season. How and why did this tradition of friendship get started?

1

It all started with a tragic disaster. On December 6, 1917, the City of Halifax, Nova Scotia was devastated by the huge detonation of a French cargo ship, fully loaded with wartime explosives, that had accidentally collided with a Norwegian ship in Halifax harbour. Approximately 1500 people were killed instantly, another 500 people died shortly after from wounds caused by debris, fires, or collapsed buildings, and it is estimated that over 9000 people were injured.

2

The Massachusetts Committee on Public Safety received a telegram from Halifax the same afternoon, telling them that half the city of Halifax was in ruins, and that there were thousands of casualties that needed help. Immediately, the governor of Massachusetts, Samuel McCall, formed the Halifax Relief Expedition. By nightfall, a

3

relief train supplied with doctors and desperately needed material was heading north to Nova Scotia. More followed: doctors from Harvard Medical School and the Massachusetts State Guard Medical Unit set up two emergency hospitals. Non-governmental organizations, such as the Christian Scientists, sent another trainload of clothing, food, money, and medical officers.

Back in Boston, a concert featuring the Boston Symphony, opera singer Nellie Melba, and violinist Fritz Kreisler, performed to a sellout crowd and raised thousands of dollars for the Halifax relief effort. A convoy of trucks laden with needed items was dispatched by the Massachusetts Automobile Club. The people of Boston rushed to Boston Harbour to fill a relief boat with supplies.

4

A year later, one of Nova Scotia's finest evergreens was delivered to Boston, and in 1971 the gesture became an annual tradition. Chosen by an official from the Nova Scotia Department of Natural Resources, the tree must meet the following specifications: approximately 15 metres high, medium to heavy density of branches, healthy with good colour, and a uniform shape. The tree is a "thank you" from Nova Scotians to Bostonians for their assistance following the 1917 Halifax explosion. The tree is Boston's official Christmas tree and is lit in the Boston Common throughout the holiday season.

5

Halifax: City of Promise

Halifax in 1917 wasn't just booming: it was changing rapidly. One of those changes was the harbour, the heart of the city and its reason for being. It had never been so busy.

Halifax was founded by the British military, as a fortress against French interests in the Maritimes. Since 1749 it had thrived in times of war. By 1917, three years of war in Europe had made Halifax a boom town. With a population of about 50 000, it was the largest in Atlantic Canada. It prided itself on keeping up with all the latest developments of the new century.

Across the harbour in Dartmouth, the pre-war town of 6500 had grown too. Three ferries were hard pressed to keep up with traffic between the two communities. On both sides of the harbour, business and industry were booming as factories, foundries and mills met the demands of a wartime economy. Everything in Halifax revolved around the harbour, the reason for the city's existence.

10

1 Nellie Melba was involved in

  a   forming the Halifax Relief Expedition.

  b   raising funds for the relief.

  c   dispatching doctors and medical personnel to Halifax.

  b   organizing a convoy of trucks to send supplies to Halifax.

2 Which of the following organizations was not involved in the relief?

  a   the Massachusetts State Guard Medical Unit

  b   Boston Symphony

  c   Nova Scotia Department of Natural Resources

  d   the Christian Scientists

3 Which of the following statements about Halifax is true?

  a   Halifax harbour was completely destroyed in the explosion.

  b   Halifax was discovered by the British in 1749.

  c   A French military ship exploded in Halifax harbour in 1917.

  d   A Norwegian ship was involved in the Halifax harbour explosion.

4 Which of the following statements about Halifax in 1917 is NOT true?

  a   Economic activities is centred upon Halifax harbour.

  b   Making supplies for the war fuelled Halifax's economic growth.

  c   Darmouth had a smaller population than Halifax.

  d   Halifax was the largest city in Canada.

5   Which of the following is the theme of paragraph 5 of the text?

   a   Boston shows great appreciation for Nova Scotia's "thank you" Christmas tree.

   b   Since 1971, Nova Scotia has sent a carefully-chosen evergreen to Boston as a token of appreciation for their assistance.

   c   Nova Scotia Department of Natural Resources ensures that only the finest evergreen is given to Boston.

   d   The annual tradition of sending an evergreen to Boston started in 1971.

6   Read "Halifax: City of Promise" in the box. Why was Halifax looked upon as a "City of Promise"?

   a   It was growing rapidly in both economy and population.

   b   It played an important role in the war.

   c   It led to the rapid growth of Dartmouth across the harbour.

   d   It was a fortress against French interests.

7   Apart from sending medical assistance and other supplies to Halifax, explain how Bostonians helped in the aftermath of the Halifax harbour explosion. Use information from the text and your own ideas to support your answer.

_____

_____

_____

_____

_____

_____

1 Your school is organizing a "Save Our Earth" week.

Write an article for the School Newsletter on what we can do at school and at home to help reduce the consumption of energy. Explain why this can help save the Earth.

──────────────── **Ideas for My Article** ────────────────

REMEMBER: *check your spelling, grammar, and punctuation.*

2 Which of the following words is misspelled?

a accommodation

b independance

c prolific

d meagre

3 Read the sentence below.

The two boys stared at _____ without saying a word.

Which word or phrase correctly completes the sentence?

a either one

b each other

c one another

d himself

4 Read the sentences below.

There are two more months to go. We still have plenty of time to complete the project.

Which of the following is the best way to combine the two sentences using a subordinate clause?

a We still have plenty of time to complete the project because there are two more months to go.

b There are two more months to go and we still have plenty of time to complete the project.

c Being two more months to go, we still have plenty of time to complete the project.

d We still have plenty of time to complete the project so there are two more months to go.

5 Read the sentence below.

_____ these two vases, I think that the _____ one is _____.

Which group of words correctly completes the sentence?

a   In, small, more eye-catching

b   Between, big, more eye-catching

c   Among, small, the most eye-catching

d   With, bigger, the most-catching

6 Read the sentence below.

This morning as I was walking to school, I saw a dog _____ across the road and was almost _____ down by a car.

Which pair of words correctly completes the sentence?

a   dash, knocking

b   dashed, knocks

c   dash, knocked

d   dashing, knocking

7 Which of the following sentences is punctuated correctly?

a   There are three simple ways to be environmentally-friendly, recycle, reuse, and reduce.

b   There are three simple ways to be environmentally-friendly; recycle, reuse, and reduce.

c   There are three simple ways to be environmentally-friendly. Recycle. Reuse, and reduce.

d   There are three simple ways to be environmentally-friendly: recycle, reuse, and reduce.

1 In helping your grandmother clean up the attic, you discovered an old chest. Describe what was inside and what you would do about it.

───────────── **Ideas for My Article** ─────────────

2 Read the sentence below.

Samantha pleaded, "_____"

Which of the following best completes the sentence?

a   Let's give it a try.

b   Let me go, please.

c   You shouldn't let him leave.

d   Go away!

3 Read the sentence below.

If he _____ about it, he _____ for help.

Which of the following verbs correctly complete the sentence?

a   knows, will have asked

b   knew, would have asked

c   had known, would have asked

d   had been knowing, would be asking

4 Read the sentence below.

By the time we _____ at the gym, all the athletes _____.

Which of the following verbs correctly complete the sentence?

a   had arrived, had gone

b   arrive, have been gone

c   arrive, have gone

d   arrived, had gone

5 Which of the following words is an antonym of the word "costly"?

a   expensive

b   cheap

c   costlier

d   cost

6 Which of the following words is a homonym of the word "waste"?

a   spend

b   waist

c   taste

d   save

7 Which of the following words is a synonym of the word "irate"?

a   angry

b   excited

c   depressed

d   puzzled

8 Read the sentence below.

_____ asking _____ book this is?

Which pair of words correctly completes the sentence?

a   Who's, whose

b   Who's, who's

c   Whose, who's

d   Whose, whose

1 Read the newspaper headline below. Think about what might be in the article that follows it. Write the article that follows the headline.

Multicultural Community Festival a Great Success

─────── **Ideas for My Newspaper Article** ───────

Multicultural Community Festival a Great Success

2 Read the sentence below.

_____ unfortunate that my dog injured _____ tail while playing around in the kitchen.

Which pair of words correctly completes the sentence?

a   Its, its

b   It's, it's

c   It's, its

d   Its, it's

3 Read the sentence below.

They _____ the airport only to find that the plane _____ off.

Which of the following correctly complete the sentence?

a   reach, takes

b   had reached, had taken

c   reached, taking

d   reached, had taken

4 Which word is not a compound word?

a   potluck

b   potbelly

c   potpourri

d   pothole

5   Which word is a homonym of "weigh"?

   a   wave

   b   heavy

   c   sleigh

   d   way

6   Which word is an antonym of "spectacular"?

   a   amazing

   b   boring

   c   wonderful

   d   spectacle

7   Read the pair of sentences below.

The man turns out to be the owner of the restaurant. I have met the man before.

Which is the best way to combine the sentences?

   a   The man, who turns out to be the owner of the restaurant, have met me before.

   b   I have met the man before and he turns out to be the owner of the restaurant.

   c   The man, whom I have met before, turns out to be the owner of the restaurant.

   d   I have met the man before as he turns out to be the owner of the restaurant.

1 Your class is going to entertain the elderly at a seniors' home near your school on Saturday evening. Suggest three events that you think the elderly would enjoy. Explain why you think so.

———————————— **Ideas for My Writing** ————————————

4

2 Which of the words below is spelled correctly?

a   resusitate

b   recuparate

c   regenerate

d   revigerate

3 Which of the words below is misspelled?

a   prototype

b   propellar

c   propaganda

d   proponent

4 Which word below is a synonym of the word "expire"?

a   expiry

b   wire

c   commence

d   end

5 Which word below is a compound word?

a   treading

b   tremendous

c   trendsetting

d   trespassing

6 Read the sentences below.

They heard the news. They hurried to the hospital. They could not find any patient by the name of Howard Grant.

Which of the following is the best way to combine the sentences?

a   After hearing the news, they hurried to the hospital but could not find any patient by the name of Howard Grant.

b   They heard the news and they hurried to the hospital and they could not find any patient by the name of Howard Grant.

c   They could not find any patient by the name of Howard Grant after hearing the news when they hurried to the hospital.

d   They heard the news and when they hurried to the hospital and they could not find any patient by the name of Howard Grant.

7 Read the sentence below.

It _____ years since we last _____ this place.

Which of the following correctly complete the sentence?

a   is, visit

b   has been, have visited

c   was, visited

d   has been, visited

8 Which of the following is punctuated correctly?

a   "Get out," the man shouted at Lou, "I don't want to see you again!"

b   Get out! The man shouted at Lou. "I don't want to see you again."

c   "Get out!" The man shouted at Lou. I don't want to see you again.

d   "Get out!" the man shouted at Lou. "I don't want to see you again."

LANGUAGE

Assessment of Reading and Writing

Grade

6

Olympics – Then and Now

In August 2004, the Olympic Games returned to their birthplace of Athens, Greece. Over 2000 years ago, athletes from all over Greece gathered at the Olympia Stadium to honour the supreme god, Zeus, and to demonstrate their agility and strength. There, they competed in the Pentathlon, which included five different events. It was at these original Olympics that the Marathon, a race of 46 kilometres, was born and continues to be one of the events in modern-day Olympics. Winners were revered and received garlands and crowns of olive branches.

1

The modern version of the Olympic Games began in Athens in 1896, after a lapse of almost 1500 years. Athletes from 14 nations were represented, with the majority of delegates from Greece, Germany, and France. An American, James Connolly, won the triple jump, making him the first Olympic champion in over 1500 years.

2

The Paris Olympics, held in 1900, were part of the Paris World Fair. These Olympic Games are particularly memorable because they marked the first appearance of female athletes at the Games.

3

Over the past 108 years, the Olympics have been held in cities all over the world, from Melbourne, Australia to Los Angeles, California and Rome, Italy to Tokyo, Japan.

4

The Olympics have not been without their problems, though. There have been acts of terrorism at some of the Games, like the 1996 Atlanta Olympics, where a terrorist bomb killed one person and injured 110 others. Other Olympic Games have been marred by steroid drug use by some athletes, forcing competitors to be eliminated and sent home in disgrace. Overall, though, even these Olympics will be best remembered for their sporting achievements.

5

The 2004 Olympic Games in Athens had more than 10 000 athletes from all over the world competing in 38 venues. Soon in 2008 it will be Beijing's turn to host the Olympics.

6

Events in 2008 Olympics

The events for the Beijing 2008 Games are quite similar to those of the Athens Games held in 2004. The 2008 Olympics will see the return of 28 sports, and will hold 302 events (165 men's events, 127 women's events, and 10 mixed events), one more event in total than in Athens.

Nine new events will be held overall, including two from the new cycling discipline of BMX. Women will compete in the 3000-metre steeplechase for the first time. In addition, marathon swimming events for men and women, over the distance of 10 kilometres, will be added to the swimming discipline. Team events (men and women) in table tennis will replace the doubles events. In fencing, women's team foil and women's team sabre will replace men's team foil and women's team epee.

1 In the earliest Olympics, athletes competed

    a   in the Marathon alone.

    b   at the Olympia Stadium.

    c   to show their passion for their countries.

    d   to win the crowns of olive branches from Zeus.

2 Which of the following statements is true?

    a   The 1896 Olympics was the first ever Olympics held in Athens.

    b   Paris hosted the Olympics in 1900 together with the Paris World Fair.

    c   There were 14 nations joining the 1900 Olympics.

    d   The 1896 Olympics saw the appearance of female and male athletes in the same events.

3 In the 1896 Athens Olympics,

    a   female athletes were allowed to compete.

    b   only athletes from Greece, Germany, and France joined the events.

    c   an American won the first championship.

    d   James Connolly became the first American to take part in the Olympic Games.

4 What is the theme of paragraph 5 of the text?

    a   Problems aside, the Olympic games are still remembered for their sporting excellence.

    b   Terrorism and drug use plagued some Olympic games.

    c   It is difficult to hold the Olympic games without any glitches.

    d   Overall, the Olympic games have been impressive.

5 In the 2004 Athens Olympics, there were

    a   27 sports.

    b   28 sports.

    c   302 events.

    d   303 events.

6 Which of the following is NOT a new event in the 2008 Beijing Olympics?

    a   doubles events in table tennis

    b   team events in table tennis

    c   women's team foil in fencing

    d   3000-metre steeplechase for women

7 How different was the 2004 Athens Olympics from the 1896 one? Use information from the text and your own ideas to answer the question.

_____

_____

_____

_____

_____

8 One Saturday afternoon as you were playing baseball with two friends in the baseball diamond next to your school, three teenagers approached you. Write what happened next.

────────── **Ideas for My Writing** ──────────

My Writing

9 Which word is an antonym of the word "postpone"?

a   advance

b   delay

c   defer

d   cone

10 Read the sentence below.

They _____ to visit their grandparents before _____ home every Saturday but now they _____ so because their grandparents _____ to live with them.

Which of the following verbs correctly complete the sentence?

a   used, going, have not done, moved

b   are used, go, do not do, have moved

c   used, going, do not do, have moved

d   have used, going, are not doing, are moving

11 Read the sentence below.

The woman sighed and said, "_____"

Which of the following best completes the sentence?

a   I wish it never happened.

b   How did it happen?

c   Lucky you!

d   It happened so fast that no one knew what to do.

12 Read the group of sentences below.

He mistakenly pushed the red button.

The door of the vault closed.

His two accomplices were locked up inside.

Which of the following is the best way to combine the sentences?

a   He mistakenly pushed the red button and the door of the vault closed and his two accomplices were locked up inside.

b   His two accomplices were locked up inside because the door of the vault closed when he mistakenly pushed the red button.

c   Because he mistakenly pushed the red button, the door of the vault closed, locking up his two accomplices inside.

d   The door of the vault closed when he mistakenly pushed the red button so that his two accomplices were locked up inside.

13 Which of the following is punctuated correctly?

a   His mother reminded him to take the following items along. A compass, a flashlight, a crank radio, no batteries needed, and a raincoat.

b   His mother reminded him to take the following items along; a compass, a flashlight, a crank radio – no batteries needed, and a raincoat.

c   His mother reminded him to take the following items along: a compass, a flashlight, a crank radio, no batteries needed, and a raincoat.

d   His mother reminded him to take the following items along: a compass, a flashlight, a crank radio (no batteries needed), and a raincoat.

The Disappearing Aral Sea

The Aral Sea in Central Asia is disappearing. It used to be the world's fourth largest lake. It had an area of 66 000 square kilometres and a volume of more than 1000 cubic kilometres. Fishermen used to have catches of 40 000 tons a year. The river deltas, marshes, and wetlands around it covered 550 000 hectares, and were once home to many fish, animal, and bird species.

1

But in the 1960s, planners in the former Soviet Union decided to make Central Asia the main supplier of raw cotton. This was not a smart decision. The land was dry, so irrigation was necessary. To these government planners, the Aral Sea seemed like a good place to get the water. The amount of irrigated land in Central Asia grew from 4.5 million hectares in 1960 to 7 million hectares 20 years later. The amount of water taken from the Aral Sea doubled. At the same time, many people moved into the area, and the population rose from 14 million to about 27 million.

2

The irrigated land became salty from using this water. Pesticides and fertilizers were used on the cotton fields, polluting the surface water and groundwater. The delta marshes and wetlands began to

3

disappear. By 1990, more than 95 per cent of the marshes and wetlands had become sandy deserts. The surface of the Aral Sea reduced in size by a half, and its volume reduced by three-quarters.

Most of the fish in the Aral Sea and the wildlife around it are now gone. In 1982, commercial fishing operations ceased. Towns and villages that used to be on the seashore are now 70 kilometres away from it. People in these communities have become sick. In the past 20 years, there has been a great increase in bronchitis as well as kidney and liver diseases. Cancer and arthritic diseases have increased by more than 60 times! The infant mortality rate in this area is near the highest in the world.   4

Scientists have spoken out strongly for saving the Aral Sea. Agricultural officials, however, say that it is impossible to demolish the canal system because too many farmers depend on the income from cotton. As an official puts it, "We could reduce by half the amount of land being irrigated. But we have to think of the people who depend on the irrigation for work. What will they do then? What will they eat?"   5

Government leaders have said that the amount of land for cotton will be reduced and large amounts of water will be pumped back into the Aral Sea. The government, however, has also indicated that the welfare of the cotton farmers must come first. Exported cotton is a major source of income.   6

Most scientists believe that the Aral Sea cannot ever be as it was before. The best they hope for is some sort of stabilization of the sea and the survival of the river's two deltas. Saving the deltas could lead to new commercial fishing activity. The five Central Asian states, who became independent countries after the former Soviet Union came apart in the 1990s, are working to solve the problems of the disappearing of the Aral Sea, through the International Fund for Saving the Aral Sea (IFAS).   7

Only time will tell if it is already too late.   8

14 Why did the delta marshes and wetlands around the Aral Sea disappear?

    a   There were too many animal and bird species living there.

    b   The irrigated land became salty.

    c   Pesticides and fertilizers were used on the cotton fields.

    d   Too much water was drained away from the Aral Sea.

15 What is the theme of paragraph 4 of the text?

    a   People started to move away from the Aral Sea because the water made them sick.

    b   The water quality of the Aral Sea led to a severe drop in the population around it.

    c   Fish and wildlife disappeared and people got sick because of the poor environment around the Aral Sea.

    d   Cancer and other diseases killed many people, including infants, around the Aral Sea.

16 Read the sentence below.

The best they hope for is some sort of stabilization of the sea and the survival of the river's two deltas.

What does the phrase "stabilization of the sea" mean?

    a   stopping the conditions of the Aral Sea from getting worse

    b   increasing the capacity of the Aral Sea

    c   improving the water quality of the Aral Sea

    d   making the water in the Aral Sea less salty

17 Which of the following statements is true?

    a   The Aral Sea used to be the fourth largest sea in the world.

    b   The Aral Sea has dried up and become cotton fields.

    c   The Aral Sea used to provide plenty of seafood.

    d   The Aral Sea covered 550 000 hectares of land at one time.

18 Read the sentence below.

Only time will tell if it is already too late.

What does the sentence mean?

    a   We need to give it more time before conditions can be improved.

    b   No one knows for sure if the Aral Sea can be saved.

    c   It is already too late to do anything about the Aral Sea.

    d   A schedule must be drawn up to make sure that actions are taken on time.

19 What are the main problems in stopping the Aral Sea from disappearing? Use information from the text and your own ideas to answer the question.

_____

_____

_____

_____

_____

20 In a garage sale, you found an ancient coin with a square hole in the centre and bought it for two dollars. When you showed it to your grandfather, he commented that it was a rare coin that might be worth a fortune. Describe what you did with it afterwards.

———————— **Ideas for My Writing** ————————

My Story

21 Read the sentence below.

_____, they had to be decisive and act fast.

Which of the following phrases best completes the sentence?

a   To defuse the crisis

b   Defusing the crisis

c   Having defused the crisis

d   Being defused the crisis

22 Which of the following sentences is correctly punctuated?

a   Thomas Edison (1847–1931) was best known for inventing the light bulb and the phonograph.

b   Thomas Edison, 1847–1931, was best known for inventing the light bulb and the phonograph.

c   Thomas Edison: 1847–1931 – was best known for inventing the light bulb, and the phonograph.

d   Thomas Edison (1847–1931); was best known for inventing the light bulb and the phonograph.

23 Read the following sentences.

Wanda doesn't enjoy fruitcake. I don't like fruitcake.

Which of the following is the best way to combine the two sentences?

a   Both Wanda and I don't enjoy fruitcake too.

b   Wanda doesn't enjoy fruitcake and neither do I.

c   Wanda doesn't enjoy fruitcake and I don't neither.

d   Wanda doesn't enjoy fruitcake and I don't enjoy it, too.

24 Which of the following is a compound word?

a   thermometer

b   permafrost

c   frostbite

d   permanent

25 Read the sentence below.

No one _____ to care what they _____. '

Which of the following verbs correctly complete the sentence?

a   seem, are doing

b   seem, do

c   is seeming, have been doing

d   seemed, had done

26 Read the following sentence.

Our teacher asked, "Are you able to come up with a solution by tomorrow?"

Which of the following is the best reported form of the sentence?

a   Our teacher asked were we able to come up with a solution by tomorrow.

b   Our teacher asked if we were able to come up with a solution by the following day.

c   Our teacher asked if we are able to come up with a solution by tomorrow.

d   Our teacher asked us to come up with a solution by the following day.

Reading Practice 1

1. b	2. a
3. c	4. a
5. d	6. a
7. b	8. b

Reading Practice 2

1. d	2. b
3. d	4. a
5. d	6. c

Reading Practice 3

1. b	2. a
3. d	4. a
5. a	6. a
7. c	

Reading Practice 4

1. c	2. a
3. c	4. a
5. c	6. a
7. b	

Reading Practice 5

1. b	2. c
3. b	4. b
5. a	6. d
7. (Individual answer)	

Reading Practice 6

1. b	2. b
3. c	4. d
5. d	
6. (Individual answer)	

Reading Practice 7

1. b	2. c
3. c	4. d
5. a	
6. (Individual answer)	

Reading Practice 8

1. b	2. c
3. b	4. a
5. d	
6. (Individual answer)	

Reading Practice 9

1. b	2. c
3. d	4. a
5. a	6. b
7. (Individual answer)	

Reading Practice 10

1. b	2. c
3. d	4. d
5. b	6. a
7. (Individual answer)	

Writing Practice 1

1. (Individual writing)
2. b   3. b
4. a   5. b
6. c   7. d

Writing Practice 2

1. (Individual writing)
2. b   3. c
4. d   5. b
6. b   7. a
8. a

Writing Practice 3

1. (Individual writing)
2. c   3. d
4. c   5. d
6. b   7. c

Writing Practice 4

1. (Individual writing)
2. c   3. b
4. d   5. c
6. a   7. d
8. d

Assessment of Reading and Writing

1. b   2. b
3. c   4. a
5. b   6. a
7. (Individual answer)
8. (Individual writing)

9. a   10. c
11. a   12. c
13. d   14. d
15. c   16. a
17. c   18. b
19. (Individual answer)
20. (Individual writing)
21. a   22. a
23. b   24. c
25. d   26. b

Contents

Test-taking **TIPS**

General

- Count the number of pages to make sure that there are no missing pages.

- Read the instructions carefully so that you know what to do and how to do it.

- Write neatly.

- Always check your answers and writing after you have completed the test.

- Skip the questions that you are stuck on and come back to them after completing the rest of the test.

MULTIPLE CHOICE

- Read through the test quickly. Skip the difficult questions and do the easy ones first.

- Read the question twice before finding the answer.

- Look for keywords in the question. (e.g. "fewer" suggests a subtraction problem; "share...equally" suggests a division problem)

- Come up with the answer in your head before looking at the possible answers.

- Read all the four options before deciding which is the correct answer.

- Eliminate the options that you know are incorrect.

PROBLEM SOLVING

- Read the whole question carefully and never make any assumptions about what the question might be.

- Highlight (i.e. underline / circle) the important information in the question.

- Translate the words into mathematical terms.

- Use drawings to help you better understand the question.

- Break down the problem into several parts and solve them one by one.

- Know exactly what needs to be included in your solution.

- Estimate the answer.

- Before writing out the solution, organize your thoughts.

- For a question that involves measurements,

  – make sure the measurements are uniform when solving the problem.
  – the measurement in the answer is converted to the unit that is asked.

- Use words to describe what you are calculating.

- Always write a concluding sentence for your solution.

- Check if your answer is reasonable (i.e. Is the answer close to your estimate?).

- Never leave a question blank. Show your work or write down your thoughts. Even if you do not get the correct answer, you might get some marks for your work.

1 Which of the following is a factor of 72 but not a composite number?

○ 36

○ 72

○ 3

○ 4

2 What does the sign below mean?

MAXIMUM

50

km/h

○ The maximum driving speed is 50 km in 1 h.

○ The maximum driving speed is 1 km in 50 h.

○ The driving speed should not be lower than 50 km/h.

○ The speed should be at least 50 km in 50 h.

3 Which is the most appropriate unit of measurement to describe the area of a beach towel?

○ cm^3

○ m^3

○ km^2

○ m^2

4 About how much water is in the jug below?

1 L

○ half a litre

○ one quarter of a litre

○ one third of a litre

○ three quarters of a litre

5 Katie buys one dress and two tops.

SALE[*]

Top ······ $8 *each*

Dress ····· $12 *each*

Pants ···· $15 *each*

[*]Buy 2 or more items and get $5 off.

How much does she need to pay?

○ $28

○ $27

○ $26

○ $23

6 Which number should be placed in the box to make the following number sentence true?

$$30 - 24 \div 2 + 1 \times 4 = \square$$

○ 22

○ 7

○ 16

○ 88

7 Look at the fractions below.

$$1\frac{1}{2} \quad \frac{5}{4} \quad \frac{4}{3} \quad 1\frac{2}{3}$$

Put the fractions in order from greatest to least.

○ $\frac{5}{4}, \frac{4}{3}, 1\frac{1}{2}, 1\frac{2}{3}$

○ $1\frac{2}{3}, \frac{4}{3}, 1\frac{1}{2}, \frac{5}{4}$

○ $1\frac{1}{2}, 1\frac{2}{3}, \frac{4}{3}, \frac{5}{4}$

○ $1\frac{2}{3}, 1\frac{1}{2}, \frac{4}{3}, \frac{5}{4}$

8 The graph below shows the number of marbles that the children have.

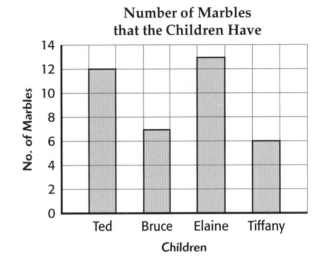

Number of Marbles that the Children Have

Which sentence is not correct?

○ Ted has more marbles than Tiffany.

○ The boys and the girls have the same number of marbles.

○ Elaine has 6 more marbles than Bruce.

○ Bruce has 5 more marbles than Ted.

9 What comes next?

○ (circle with diagonal lines, large)

○ (circle with diagonal lines, small)

○ (circle with many dots, large)

○ (circle with dots, small)

10 In K & M Grocery Store, apples are sold in groups of 3 and oranges are sold in groups of 5.

If Mrs. Winter buys 26 apples and oranges in all, how many apples does she buy? How many oranges does she buy?

Explain Your Thinking

11 Uncle Jimmy wants to lay his backyard with sod. Each piece of sod is in the shape of a rectangle that measures 1 m by 2 m. A drawing of his backyard is shown below.

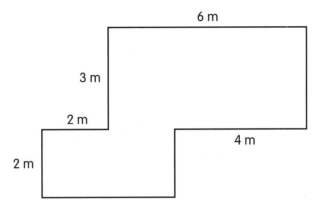

How many pieces of sod will Uncle Jimmy need to cover his backyard?

Explain Your Thinking

1 Which set of values is represented by the 4 points on the number line?

○ 2.81, 2.82, 2.85, 2.90

○ 2.85, 2.91, 2.95, 2.99

○ 2.84, 2.86, 2.90, 2.98

○ 2.90, 2.92, 2.95, 2.99

2 Which one of the following numbers is 5.6 when it is rounded to the nearest tenth, and is 5.62 when it is rounded to the nearest hundredth?

○ 5.614

○ 5.617

○ 5.628

○ 5.671

3 The following shape has an order of rotational symmetry of 2.

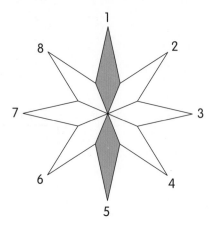

Flap 1 and flap 5 are already shaded. Which flap(s) should be shaded as well to get an order of rotational symmetry of 8?

○ 3, 7

○ 2, 4, 6, 8

○ 2, 6

○ 2, 3, 4, 6, 7, 8

4 Look at the pattern.

3, 7, 15, 31, 63...

What comes next?

○ 67

○ 79

○ 114

○ 127

5 Look at the time shown.

What time will it be after two and a half hours?

- ○ 17:38
- ○ 3:38 p.m.
- ○ 18:08
- ○ 6:08 a.m.

6 What is the volume of the triangular prism below?

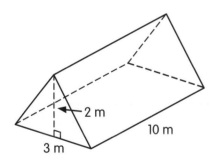

- ○ 60 m³
- ○ 15 m³
- ○ 20 m³
- ○ 30 m³

7 What is the most appropriate unit to measure the volume of a swimming pool?

- ○ cm³
- ○ m²
- ○ m³
- ○ mm³

8 Look at the grid below.

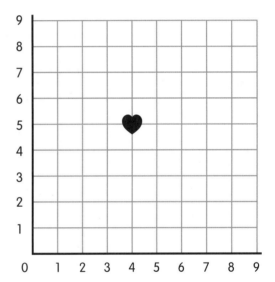

If ♥ is moved 3 units down and a few units right, which one will possibly be the new coordinates of ♥ ?

- ○ (3,2)
- ○ (6,7)
- ○ (8,2)
- ○ (8,4)

9 Plot the following points on the grid.

A(1,1)   B(6,1)

C(8,7)   D(3,7)

Join the points to see what quadrilateral is formed. Name and tell the characteristics of the quadrilateral. Then find its area.

Show Your Work

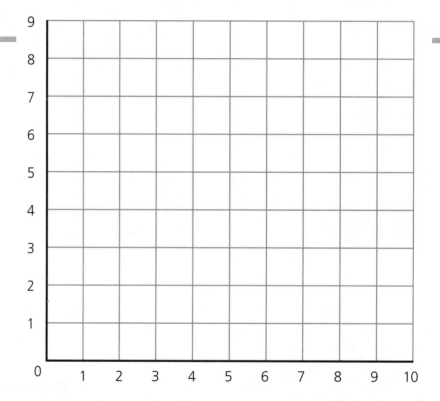

10 The members of the Environmental Club of Pineway Public School plant trees every month. They recorded the number of trees they planted in the past 9 months.

Number of Trees:

43   77   69   43   69   52   43   34   47

What are the mean, median, and mode numbers of trees they planted?

Janet is the president of the club. If she wants to write a letter to the government to apply for a fund to subsidize the environmental activities, which central tendency should she use to support her application?

Explain Your Thinking

1 Which of the following should be put on the line to make the number sentence true?

$$24 + \underline{\hspace{1cm}} \div 2 = 27$$

○ 10 – 4

○ 4 + 2

○ 18 ÷ 3

○ 32 – 2

2 A compass is at an angle of 50°.

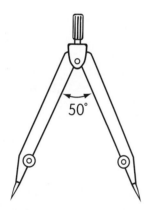

At least how many more degrees do you need to open the compass so that it shows an obtuse angle?

○ 11°

○ 21°

○ 31°

○ 41°

3 The area of the parallelogram is 30 cm².

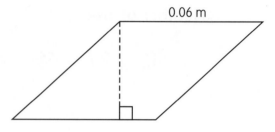

0.06 m

What is its height in centimetres?

○ 5 cm

○ 0.5 cm

○ 10 cm

○ 1 cm

4 Which pattern has this rule?

"Increase by adding the same number to each term."

○ 20, 18, 16, 14, 12

○ 5, 13, 21, 29, 37

○ 2, 3, 5, 8, 12

○ 10, 20, 40, 80, 160

5 Which shapes have the same area?

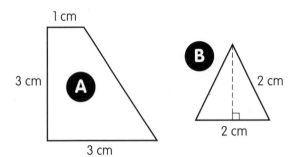

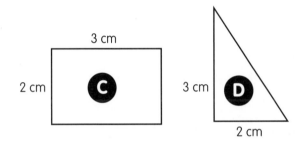

- ○ A and B
- ○ A and C
- ○ A, B, and D
- ○ B and C

6 Which set is in order from least to greatest?

- ○ 2.451, 2.415, 2.154, 2.145
- ○ 0.826, 0.862, 0.268, 0.286
- ○ 1.023, 1.203, 1.302, 1.320
- ○ 3.097, 3.079, 3.970, 3.790

7 A report shows that 92% of children watch TV every day. Which of the following number is equivalent to 92%?

- ○ 9.2
- ○ $\frac{92}{1000}$
- ○ 0.92
- ○ $\frac{0.92}{1000}$

8 What is the probability that the pointer will land on red?

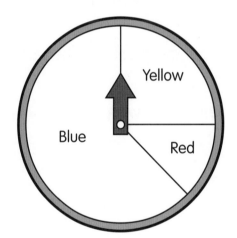

- ○ 0
- ○ $\frac{1}{3}$
- ○ $\frac{1}{4}$
- ○ $\frac{1}{8}$

9 Jill has a robot which walks at 8 cm/s at normal speed and 1 cm more in a second if it is at turbo speed.

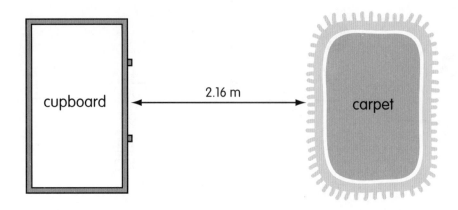

How long does it take the robot to walk from the cupboard to the carpet at normal speed?

How much time will be saved if the robot walks at turbo speed instead?

Show Your Work

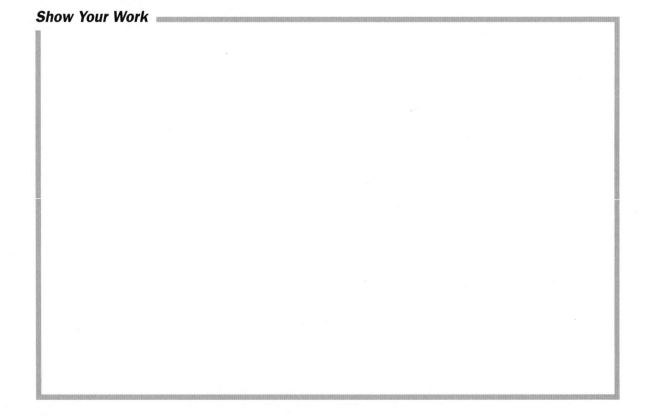

10 John makes the rectangle below with a wire.

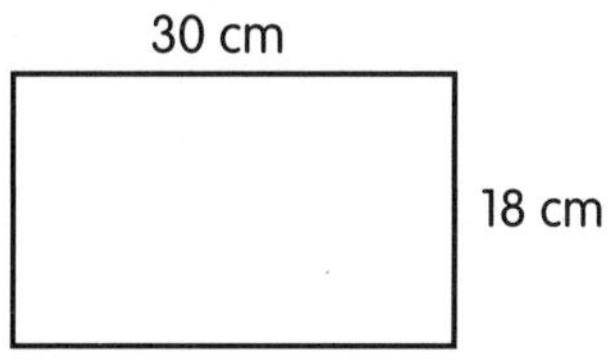

30 cm

18 cm

John uses the same wire to make a square.

What is the side length of the square?

Does the square have the same area as the rectangle? Explain.

Explain Your Thinking

1   Sam can fold two paper planes in a minute. How many paper planes can Sam fold in 4 hours?

- ○ 240
- ○ 360
- ○ 480
- ○ 600

2   Compare the areas of the two shapes below.

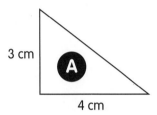

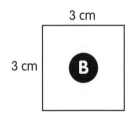

Which sentence is true?

- ○ A is larger than B by 3 cm².
- ○ B is larger than A by 3 cm².
- ○ A is larger than B by 6 cm².
- ○ B is larger than A by 6 cm².

3   Kenneth draws a ball from the bag without looking.

What is the probability of drawing a ball that is not "5"?

- ○ $\frac{6}{7}$
- ○ $\frac{1}{5}$
- ○ $\frac{4}{5}$
- ○ $\frac{1}{7}$

4   What is the sum of the number sentence below?

$$\frac{999}{999} + \frac{7}{7} + 6 = ?$$

- ○ 3
- ○ 8
- ○ 976
- ○ 1012

5 What is the sum in expanded form of the number sentence below?

$$65.23 + 125.53 = \underline{\hspace{1cm}}$$

- ○ 100 + 9 + 0.7 + 0.06
- ○ 100 + 90 + 0.7 + 0.6
- ○ 100 + 9 + 0.07 + 0.6
- ○ 100 + 90 + 0.7 + 0.06

6 If ★ = 6, what is the value of 15 + ★ x 2 ÷ 3?

- ○ 9
- ○ 14
- ○ 16
- ○ 19

7 Which pattern has the pattern rule below?

"Subtract half of the previous term."

- ○ 2, 4, 8, 16, 32
- ○ 64, 32, 16, 8, 4
- ○ 50, 48, 46, 44, 42
- ○ 25, 20, 15, 10, 5

8 Which fraction represents the shaded part of the shape below?

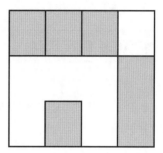

- ○ $\dfrac{1}{2}$
- ○ $\dfrac{5}{7}$
- ○ $\dfrac{5}{12}$
- ○ $\dfrac{6}{8}$

9 The following record shows the amount of water drunk by each child during lunch on a specific day.

Child	Amount of Water Drunk
A	0.58 L
B	$\dfrac{2}{5}$ L
C	510 mL
D	half a litre

Which child drank the least?

- ○ A
- ○ B
- ○ C
- ○ D

10 The table shows the number of toy cars sold by each salesperson.

	David	Tom	Amy	Karen	Winnie
No. of Toy Cars Sold	1236	1427	926	1063	1184

Make a bar graph to show the data. You may use rounded figures to complete the bar graph.

If each salesperson earns a commission of $0.70 for each toy car sold, whose commission is closest to $600?

Show Your Work

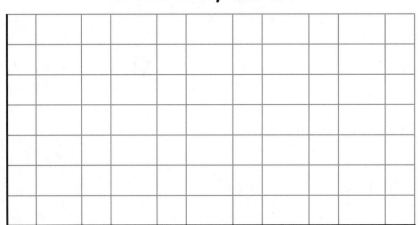

Number of Toy Cars Sold

11 Abby wants to buy a dozen eggs to make a birthday cake. She compares the costs of the eggs from two grocery stores and the costs of travelling to these stores.

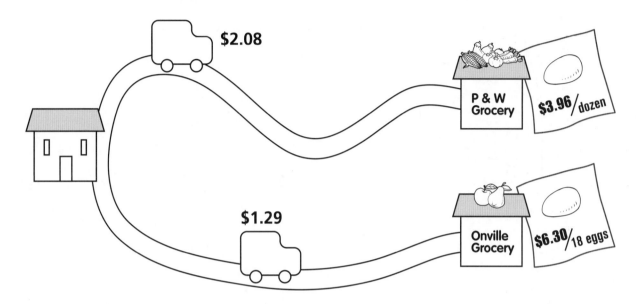

$2.08

P & W Grocery $3.96/dozen

$1.29

Onville Grocery $6.30/18 eggs

Which store should she go to buy eggs? What is the total cost?

Explain Your Thinking

1 What is the volume of the triangular block in cubic millimetres?

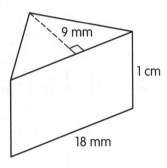

9 mm

1 cm

18 mm

○ 0.81

○ 81

○ 810

○ 1620

2 There are 48 boys and 54 girls in Grade 6 of Pineway Public School. What is the ratio of the girls to the boys in simplest form?

○ 48:54

○ 9:8

○ 27:24

○ 8:9

3 The cost of 32 bikes is the same as the cost of 128 dolls. If the cost of each doll is $16, how much is a bike?

○ $32

○ $64

○ $128

○ $256

4 Arrange the numbers from greatest to least.

200% $2\frac{7}{10}$ 1.875

○   1.875, 200%, $2\frac{7}{10}$

○   200%, $2\frac{7}{10}$, 1.875

○   200%, 1.875, $2\frac{7}{10}$

○ $2\frac{7}{10}$, 200%, 1.875

5 What is the 7th term in the number pattern?

475, 440, 405, 370...

○ 230

○ 265

○ 295

○ 300

6 Tony is measuring the perimeter of a farm using a measuring wheel.

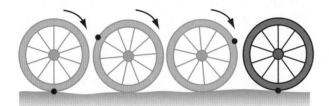

The circumference of the wheel is 2 m. How many full turns will the wheel make if the perimeter of the farm is 2.2 km?

○ 11
○ 110
○ 1100
○ 11 000

7 Last year, the highest temperature in summer was 34°C, and the lowest temperature in winter was -20°C. What is the difference between the highest and the lowest temperatures in °C?

○ 14
○ 20
○ 34
○ 54

8 Which is the top view of the solid below?

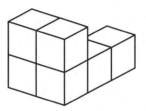

○

○

○

○

9 Which number is a factor of 60, but not a factor of 72?

○ 4
○ 6
○ 12
○ 15

10 Leo made a spinner with 16 equal sections and numbered each section from 1 to 16.

Leo lets each of his friends choose one of the guesses below before he or she spins the spinner. If the guess of the player matches the number that the pointer lands on, he or she gets a prize.

Guess 1: multiples of 4

Guess 2: greater than 10

Guess 3: factors of 10

If you are one of Leo's friends, which guess will you choose? Explain your choice.

Explain Your Thinking

11 Tom had 69 basketball cards and Jack had 24.

Tom gave some of his cards to Jack and still has 7 more cards than Jack.

How many cards did Tom give Jack? How many cards does each of them have now?

Explain Your Thinking

1 James started driving to Ottawa at 9:35 a.m. It took him 3 h 30 min to get there. What time did he arrive in Ottawa?

○ 6:05 a.m.

○ 12:05 p.m.

○ 1:05 p.m.

○ 1:25 p.m.

2 The net of a cube is shown below.

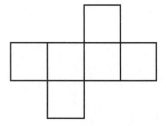

The area of the net is 24 cm². What is the side length of the cube?

○ 1 cm

○ 2 cm

○ 4 cm

○ 6 cm

3 There is $\frac{4}{5}$ of a litre of milk in a jar. If Sue pours out 250 mL of milk from the jar, how much milk will be left?

○ 550 mL

○ 450 mL

○ 250 mL

○ 150 mL

4 A survey shows that $\frac{1}{4}$ of the population has less than 5 hours of sleep a day and 45% has more than 8 hours. What is the portion of the population that has 5 to 8 hours of sleep a day?

○ $\frac{3}{4}$

○ 0.3

○ 55%

○ 0.03

5 Look at the equations.

$$n + 1 = 15$$
$$n + 1 + s = 19$$

What is the value of s?

O 2

O 3

O 4

O 5

6 The perimeter of the following rectangle is 210 cm.

0.15 m

What is the ratio of its length to its width?

O 699:1

O 12:1

O 15:14

O 6:1

7 The graph shows the time and distance travelled in Tom's journey.

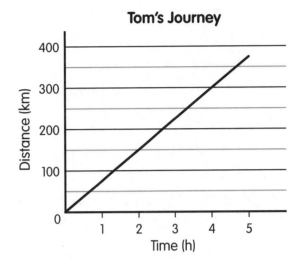

How far will Tom travel if he drives for 6 hours?

O 450 m

O 450 000 m

O 4500 km

O 45 km

8 Which number should be placed in the box to make the number sentence true?

$$3.92 - 2 \times 1.35 = \boxed{}$$

O 2.591

O 2.592

O 1.21

O 1.22

9 Louise made the triangles below with sticks and modelling clay.

1 layer

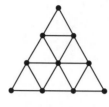

2 layers

3 layers

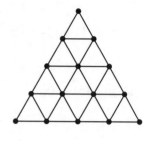

4 layers

Help her record the number of balls of modelling clay used in the chart.

Louise says, "I can make a triangle with 10 layers if I have 2 more balls of modelling clay."

How many balls of modelling clay does she have now?

No. of Layers	No. of •
1	
2	
3	
4	

Explain Your Thinking

10 Draw a triangle with vertices (7,9), (7,14), and (10,14). Then name it A.

Mark the point at (7,9) as P on the grid.

Rotate triangle A $\frac{1}{4}$ clockwise about P. Then name it B.

Explain how you would create a picture that has a rotational symmetry of 4 using triangle A.

Draw the picture on the grid and describe the transformation that you used.

Explain Your Thinking

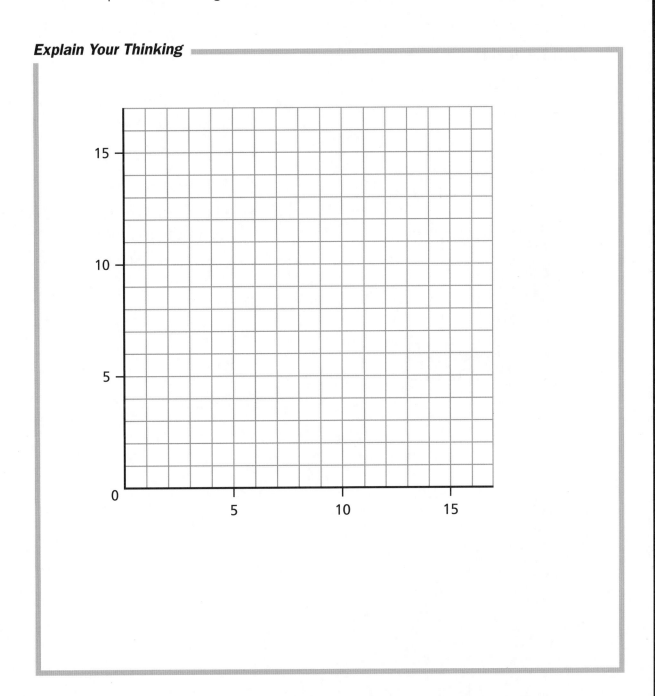

1 Which of the following is the closest estimate of the angle?

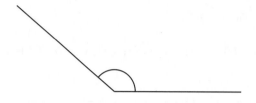

- ○ 105° to 115°
- ○ 135° to 145°
- ○ 35° to 45°
- ○ 90° to 100°

2 What fraction of the shape is shaded?

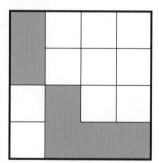

- ○ $\frac{7}{8}$
- ○ $\frac{3}{4}$
- ○ $\frac{6}{15}$
- ○ $\frac{3}{8}$

3 Jack took a train from Toronto to Montreal. The train left at 9:48 a.m. and arrived at Montreal at 2:03 p.m. How long did it take Jack to travel from Toronto to Montreal?

- ○ 4 h 5 min
- ○ 3 h 15 min
- ○ 4 h 15 min
- ○ 5 h 15 min

4 Which number matches all the descriptions below?

- • It is a prime number.
- • It is between 28 and 42.
- • The sum of its digits is a composite number.
- • It is a factor of 148.

- ○ 31
- ○ 37
- ○ 41
- ○ 74

5 A hiking area has 3 trails.

Trail	Length
A	2.81 km
B	629 m
C	2.098 km

What is the length of the longest trail expressed in metres?

○ 2098 m

○ 0.281 m

○ 281 m

○ 2810 m

6 What solid can be formed by the net below?

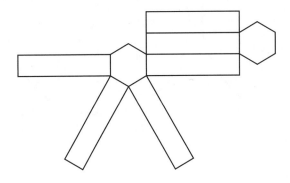

○ rectangular prism

○ pentagonal prism

○ hexagonal pyramid

○ hexagonal prism

7 Rotate the shape a quarter turn clockwise about point M.

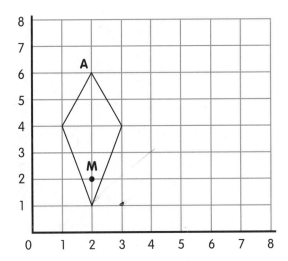

What are the new coordinates of A?

○ (8,0)

○ (7,1)

○ (6,2)

○ (5,3)

8 Coach Samson wants to rearrange 169 scouts into rows. Each row has the same number of scouts. Which way can Coach Samson use to rearrange the scouts?

○ 9 rows of 16 scouts

○ 13 rows of 13 scouts

○ 16 rows of 9 scouts

○ 21 rows of 7 scouts

9 Jack volunteers to help his teacher make spinners for the school fair. His teacher made a chart to record details of the spinners and asked Jack to make two of the three spinners.

Spinner*	Red	Green	Blue
A	$\frac{1}{8}$	$\frac{1}{4}$	$\frac{5}{8}$
B	$\frac{1}{8}$	$\frac{1}{2}$	$\frac{3}{8}$
C	$\frac{3}{8}$	$\frac{1}{2}$	$\frac{1}{8}$

*The player will win a toy if the pointer lands on red or green.

Label the two spinners that Jack has made.

If you play this game, which spinner will you choose to spin?

Explain Your Thinking

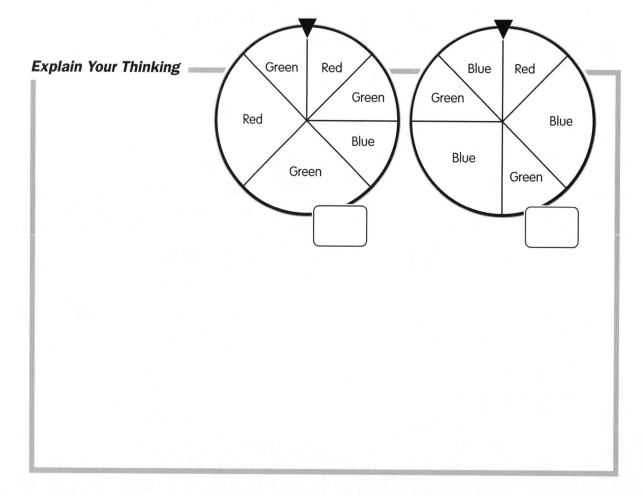

10 Look at the fenced rectangular plot in Jenny's backyard.

3 m

2 m

Jenny wants to double the length and the width of the existing rectangular plot. She thinks that the amount of fencing needed will double too. Is she correct?

Jenny then decides to seed her new backyard with grass seeds. If it takes two bags of grass seeds to cover the old plot, how many bags of grass seeds are needed to cover the new plot?

Explain Your Thinking

1 A bag of gumballs is shown below.

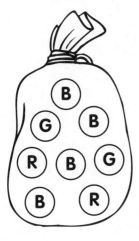

*R = Red
B = Blue
G = Green

Which sentence is not true?

- ○ It is more likely to draw red than green.

- ○ Blue has the greatest chance to be drawn.

- ○ Red has less chance to be drawn than blue.

- ○ It is equally likely to draw red and green.

2 Joseph walks 7.8 m in 6 s. How fast does he walk?

- ○ 0.13 m/s
- ○ 1.3 cm/s
- ○ 130 cm/s
- ○ 13 000 mm/s

3 What is the perimeter of the triangle?

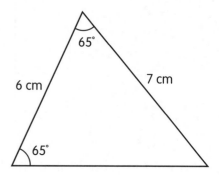

- ○ 16.5 cm
- ○ 18 cm
- ○ 19 cm
- ○ 20 cm

4 What is the smallest 4-digit number that can be formed with 0, 1, 3, 6?

- ○ 1306
- ○ 1036
- ○ 1006
- ○ 6310

5 If Bob drives at 58 km/h for 2 hours and 62 km/h for another hour, how far will he travel?

○ 120 km

○ 186 km

○ 174 km

○ 178 km

6 Which set of values is represented by the 4 points on the number line?

1.3   1.5

○ 1.32, 1.38, 1.4, 1.45

○ 1.31, 1.34, 1.35, 1.4

○ 1.302, 1.309, 1.4, 1.405

○ 1.31, 1.314, 1.315, 1.41

7 Eighteen blocks measuring 4 cm by 2 cm by 2 cm fit into the rectangular prism perfectly.

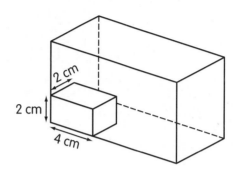

What is the volume of the rectangular prism in cubic centimetres?

○ 72 cm^3

○ 144 cm^3

○ 192 cm^3

○ 288 cm^3

8 Josephine's father is 43 years and 4 months old. How old is he in months?

○ 516

○ 520

○ 47

○ 564

9 Sue has made an input-output machine. When the input number is 9, the output number is 56.

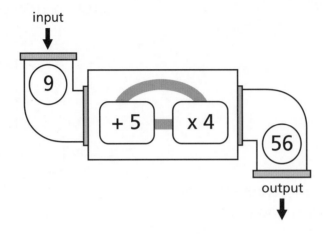

Write 3 input numbers and find the corresponding output numbers.

Then design a similar machine that works in a reverse direction. Use the same pair of input and output numbers as above in your design.

Show Your Work

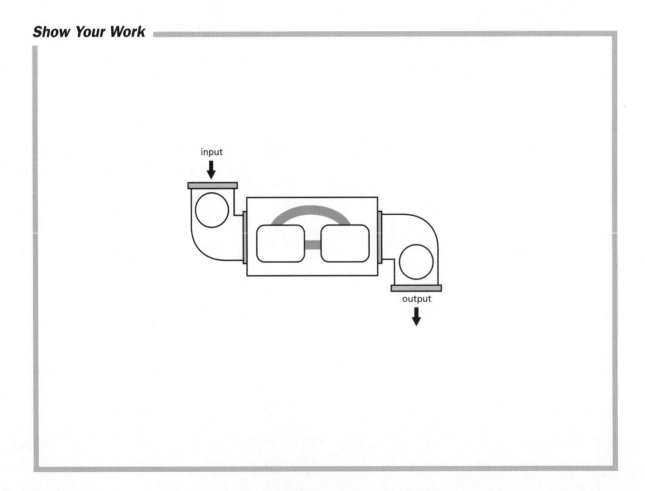

10 Jason is in Town A. He wants to go to Town C through Town B.

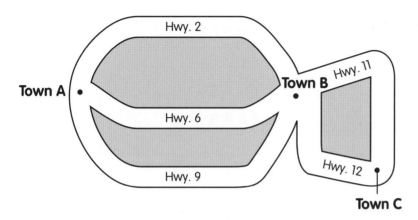

Highway	Length
2	273.14 km
6	203.55 km
9	224.36 km
11	146.45 km
12	176.86 km

Draw a tree diagram to show all the possible routes that Jason can take. Suggest the shortest route to him.

Show Your Work

1 A food bank collected 360 cans of food last month. Sarah helped put the cans equally into 45 boxes. How many cans are there in each box?

○ 6

○ 7

○ 8

○ 9

2 A farmer wants to plant trees around his farm. The dimensions of his farm are as follows:

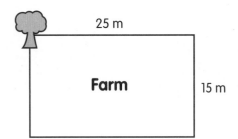

25 m

Farm

15 m

If the distance from one tree to the next is 5 m, how many trees does the farmer need?

○ 8

○ 14

○ 16

○ 78

3 Which of the following is equivalent to $\frac{9}{20}$?

○ 0.018

○ 45%

○ 4.5%

○ 1.8

4 Two bags of candies weigh $2\frac{5}{8}$ kg and $1\frac{7}{8}$ kg. The candies are put into a jar that weighs $\frac{1}{8}$ kg. What is the weight of a jar of candies in total?

○ $3\frac{3}{8}$ kg

○ $3\frac{5}{8}$ kg

○ $4\frac{5}{8}$ kg

○ $4\frac{6}{8}$ kg

5 Leo is 7 years old. His age is 2 times Katie's plus 1. How old is Katie?

- ○ 3 years old
- ○ 4 years old
- ○ 13 years old
- ○ 15 years old

6 Christine has 2 strips of ribbon. If one is 8.273 m long and the other is 4.876 m longer, how much ribbon does she have in all?

- ○ 13.149 m
- ○ 11.67 m
- ○ 18.025 m
- ○ 21.422 m

7 Susanna spent $10 on candies, $25 on movie tickets, and $15 on magazines today. The total amount she spent is 25% of her weekly income. What is her daily earning if she works on weekdays only?

- ○ $2.50
- ○ $150
- ○ $250
- ○ $40

8 What is the name of the triangle below?

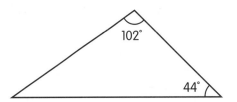

- ○ acute isosceles triangle
- ○ obtuse scalene triangle
- ○ right scalene triangle
- ○ obtuse isosceles triangle

9 EasyWrite Pen Factory produces 642 boxes of pens a day. How many boxes of pens does the factory produce in 8 weeks if it closes on weekends?

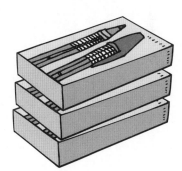

- ○ 5136
- ○ 25 680
- ○ 30 816
- ○ 35 952

10 Mrs. Smith recorded the sales of strawberry cakes last year.

Number of Strawberry Cakes Sold

Jan	Feb	Mar	Apr
250	200	325	450
May	Jun	Jul	Aug
350	400	350	550
Sep	Oct	Nov	Dec
675	425	425	400

Graph the data.

Which months' sales are higher than the average monthly sales?

Show Your Work

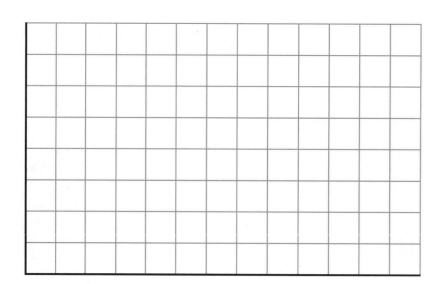

11 Adam is making a net for a 3-dimensional figure.

Draw the missing face to complete the net.

Draw the 3-dimensional figure that is formed by the net on the grid.

Describe the figure to tell about the following:

- number of vertices and edges

- shapes of the faces

Show Your Work

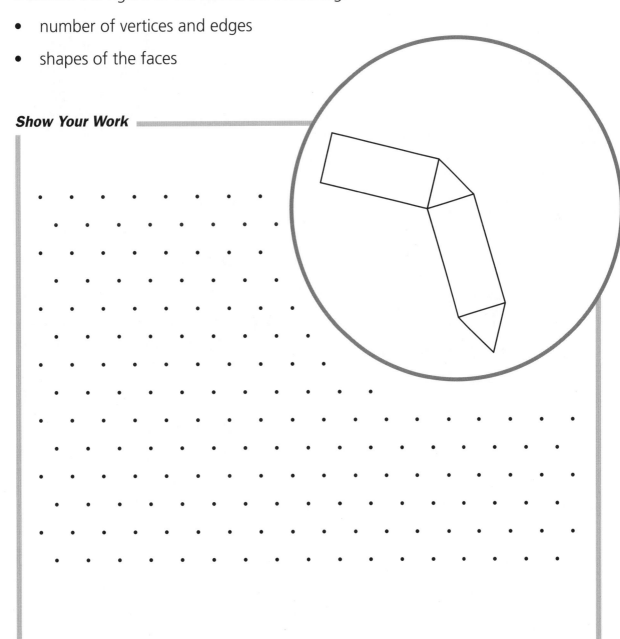

1 Which of the following is equivalent to 0.4?

○ $\frac{4}{100}$

○ $\frac{1}{25}$

○ $\frac{2}{5}$

○ $\frac{3}{5}$

2 Mary has made a special drink which contains 355 mL of iced tea and 1.53 L of juice. How much drink has Mary made?

○ 0.1885 L

○ 354.53 mL

○ 1.885 L

○ 5.08 L

3 Ken and Pauline made a total of 192 cookies for fundraising. If the number of cookies that Ken made is half the number that Pauline made, how many cookies did Ken make?

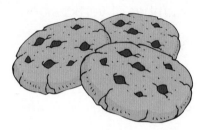

○ 32

○ 64

○ 128

○ 256

4 A regular polygon has a side length of 6 cm and a perimeter of 30 cm. What polygon is it?

○ square

○ rectangle

○ pentagon

○ hexagon

5 What is the volume of the solid below?

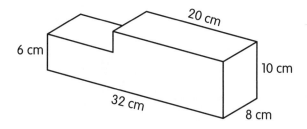

- ○ 1536 cm³
- ○ 2176 cm³
- ○ 2478 cm³
- ○ 2560 cm³

6 Robert had $50 in quarters. He spent $4.50 for a bag of chips and $7.68 for a movie ticket. How many quarters did he have left?

- ○ 151
- ○ 249
- ○ 755
- ○ 1245

7 Which shape has the following characteristics?

- It has 4 sides.
- It has 2 acute angles and 2 obtuse angles.
- It has one pair of parallel lines only.

- ○ parallelogram
- ○ square
- ○ rhombus
- ○ trapezoid

8 About what percent of the shape below is shaded?

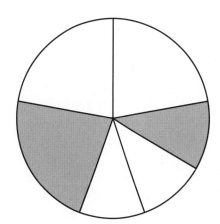

- ○ 40%
- ○ 0.3
- ○ 33%
- ○ 50%

9 Each student in Mrs. Duncan's class draws a triangle. Erica's and Tina's triangles are shown in the circle.

David followed the descriptions below to draw another triangle.

- ∠ABC = 72°

- BC = 8 cm

- Join the points A and C.

Draw David's triangle with the given line AB.

Which girl's triangle is similar to David's? Explain.

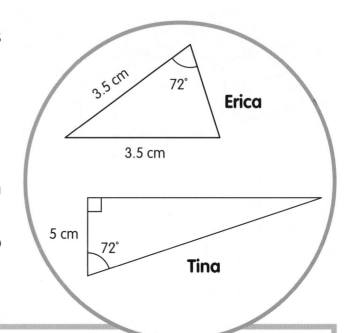

Show Your Work

A ——————————— B

10 Katie recorded the marks she got on her math quizzes in a chart.

Quiz*	Mark
1	78
2	
3	85
4	69
5	74

*Each quiz is out of 100.

Katie spilled some chocolate milk on the chart by accident. The spill covered the mark of her second quiz.

The average mark of her quizzes is 79.

What did Katie get on her second quiz?

Is it possible for Katie to have an average of 85 if she has one more quiz?

Explain Your Thinking

1 Two spinners are spun at the same time.

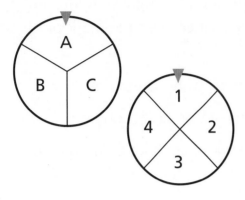

How many possible outcomes will there be?

○ 7

○ 9

○ 12

○ 18

2 Karen has a hobby of collecting nickels. If Karen's goal is to have nickels that are worth $10 000, how many nickels will there be in her collection?

○ 20 000

○ 50 000

○ 100 000

○ 200 000

3 Which pattern has the rule below?

"Decrease by subtracting the same number from each term."

○ 48, 24, 12, 6, 3

○ 48, 44, 40, 36, 32

○ 48, 46, 50, 48, 52

○ 48, 40, 31, 21, 10

4 Which sentence is true about the triangle below?

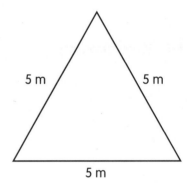

○ It has an obtuse angle.

○ It is a right-angle triangle.

○ Each angle is 60°.

○ The angles are in different sizes, but their sum is 180°.

5 Which number are the following sentences describing?

- It is between 33 and 39.
- It is a composite number.
- 5 is not a factor of it.

- ○ 26
- ○ 35
- ○ 36
- ○ 37

6 Joe wants to buy a dining set and an armchair which cost $2992.36 and $813.57 respectively. The tax for these items is $532.83. About how much does Joe need to pay in total?

- ○ $3100
- ○ $3300
- ○ $4100
- ○ $4300

7 Jack draws three vertices of a square on the Cartesian plane below.

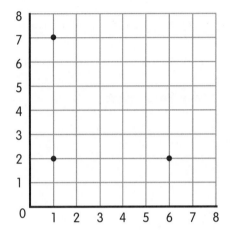

What are the coordinates of the missing vertex?

- ○ (4,6)
- ○ (5,7)
- ○ (6,7)
- ○ (7,6)

8 It is 10:27 a.m. now. What time will it be after 4 hours 38 minutes?

- ○ 13:05
- ○ 3:05 p.m.
- ○ 16:05
- ○ 2:05 p.m.

9 Jason uses sixteen 1-cm sticks to make different rectangles. How many different rectangles can he make?

Which rectangle has the greatest area?

Use diagrams to illustrate your answer.

Show Your Work

10 Mrs. Green had prepared some fruit punch for her family gathering. Each jar contained 8 cups of fruit punch. Mrs. Green's son, Johnny, recorded the number of cups each person drank in the chart below.

Family Member	Grandma	Grandpa	Mom	Dad	Johnny
Number of Cups Drunk	2	3	3	5	4

How many jars of fruit punch did they drink in all? Express your answer as fraction.

Show Your Work

1 Which of the following is equivalent to 121%?

○ $12\frac{1}{100}$

○ 0.121

○ $\frac{121}{1000}$

○ 1.21

2 Ivan has a bag of candies in different colours:

- 4 red
- 5 green
- 5 blue
- 7 yellow

Ivan took out a red candy from the bag. If he takes out another candy without looking, what is the probability that the candy he picks is green?

○ $\frac{5}{21}$

○ $\frac{5}{20}$

○ $\frac{3}{20}$

○ $\frac{5}{19}$

3 How many grams of pasta are in one serving if 1.5 kg of pasta can serve 6 people?

○ 0.25 g

○ 25 g

○ 250 g

○ 2500 g

4 Which statement best describes the transformation from △IJK to △MLK?

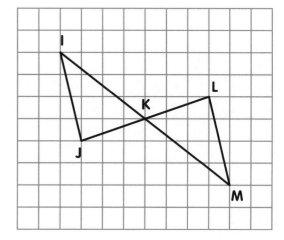

○ Make a $\frac{1}{4}$ turn clockwise about point K.

○ Reflect in line JK.

○ Make a $\frac{1}{2}$ turn about point K.

○ Reflect about point K.

5 The data below shows the number of babies born in a city each day in the past 5 days.

21, 90, 17, 83, 79

How many babies were born each day on average?

O 54

O 56

O 58

O 62

6 What is the total surface area of the rectangular prism below in m² ?

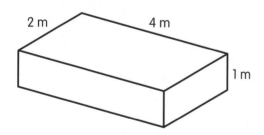

O 8

O 14

O 28

O 48

7 The circle graph below shows the number of hours Tommy spends on different activities in a day.

Time Spent on Different Activities

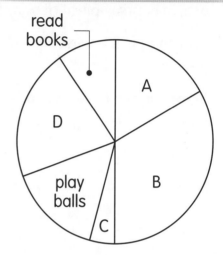

Tommy sleeps 8 hours a day. Which section represents the amount of time he spends on sleeping?

O A

O B

O C

O D

8 Which number below is a factor of 50 but not a composite number?

O 2

O 7

O 10

O 25

9 Ashley drew a polygon on the board. She describes the polygon as follows:

- ∠DAB = 60° and DA = 4 cm

- ∠CBA = 60° and CB = 4 cm

What is the shape of the polygon ABCD?

Ashley bends a piece of wire to form the shape of polygon ABCD.

How long is the wire?

Show Your Work

A ——————————————— B

10 There are 6 rounds in a game. Look at the scores that Alan got in the first 4 rounds of the game.

If the mean, median, and mode of the player's scores are the same, then the player will win a prize.

Suggest one set of scores that Alan should get in the 5th and 6th rounds, so that he can win a prize.

Alan's Score

Round	Score
1	75
2	53
3	62
4	68
5	
6	

Explain Your Thinking

1 Which of the following is not equivalent to 3:5?

○ 6:10

○ 15:20

○ 30:50

○ 36:60

2 The graph shows the distance that Mr. Brown travelled on his trip to a cottage.

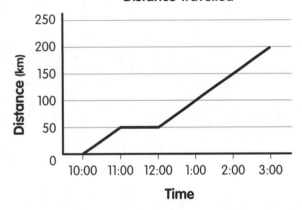

Distance Travelled

Mr. Brown made a stop for lunch. When was Mr. Brown having his lunch?

○   10:00 – 11:00

○   10:00 – 12:00

○   11:00 – 12:00

○   12:00 – 1:00

3 Each set of values below shows the lengths of the 3 sides of a triangle. Which set of value is the side length of an isosceles triangle?

○ 3, 4, 5

○ 2, 3, 2

○ 5, 5, 5

○ 3, 1, 4

4 Jane practises $\frac{3}{4}$ h of piano on every Monday, and $1\frac{1}{2}$ h on every Tuesday and Wednesday. How many minutes does she practise piano each week?

○ $1\frac{1}{4}$

○ $3\frac{3}{4}$

○ 135

○ 225

5 Tom is 1.78 m tall. Howard is taller than Tom but shorter than 2 m. How tall might Howard be?

○ 176 cm

○ 184 cm

○ 2.84 m

○ 207 cm

6 Look at the rectangular carpet.

1.5 m

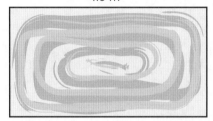

If the perimeter of the carpet is 460 cm, what is its area in m^2?

○ 8

○ 306

○ 1.2

○ 4.65

7 The table shows the number of candies Mary's robot ate on the 3rd, 4th, 5th, and 6th days last week.

Day	No. of Candies
.	.
.	.
.	.
3rd	9
4th	16
5th	25
6th	36
.	.
.	.
.	.

How many candies did Mary's robot eat on the 1st, 2nd, and 7th days?

○ 1 ; 4 ; 49

○ 1 ; 2 ; 45

○ 2 ; 5 ; 47

○ 3 ; 6 ; 48

8 What is the missing number?

$$35 - 28 \div 7 \times \boxed{} = 27$$

○ 0

○ 1

○ 2

○ 27

9 Jason designs a pattern with a roll of string and records the side length of each square.

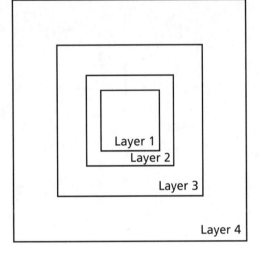

Layer	Side Length (cm)
1	2
2	3
3	5
4	8

The roll of string is 2.5 m long.

How many layers at most will there be in Jason's design?

Explain Your Thinking

10 Jessica has asked 25 children about their favourite lunch.

She organized the data and recorded the result in the chart.

Our Favourite Lunch

Pizza	40%
Sandwich	20%
Burger	29%
Others	18%

Is the result reasonable? Explain.

Assume that the result for "sandwich" is correct. How many children choose sandwich as their favourite lunch?

Explain Your Thinking

1 Which number are the sentences describing?

- It is a composite number.
- It has 4 factors.
- The sum of its digits is a prime number.
- It is not a factor of 42.

○ 21

○ 34

○ 36

○ 48

2 A 12-g box contains 18 chocolate bars. If each chocolate bar weighs 117 g, how heavy is a box of chocolate bar?

○ 2 kg 106 g

○ 2118 kg

○ 2 kg 118 g

○ 2116 kg

3 Sam has 2570 eggs. If each carton holds a dozen eggs, how many more eggs are needed to fill up the last carton?

○ 2

○ 8

○ 10

○ 12

4 The distance between Judy's house and Oakfield via Clingtown is 360 km.

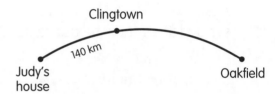

Clingtown

140 km

Judy's house

Oakfield

Judy arrives at Clingtown by train. If she takes a bus which travels at 55 km/h to finish off the journey, how long will it take her?

○ 3 h

○ 4 h

○ 5 h

○ 6 h

5 Find the area of the L-shape figure below.

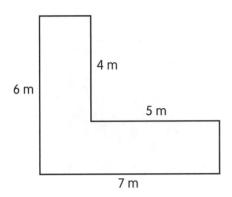

- ○ 20 m^2
- ○ 22 m^2
- ○ 24 m^2
- ○ 26 m^2

6 Justin wants to have a sandwich for lunch. The food stall serves two choices of bread and three choices of meat. How many combinations are there?

- ○ 3
- ○ 4
- ○ 5
- ○ 6

7 Triangle ABC has been transformed to triangle PQR.

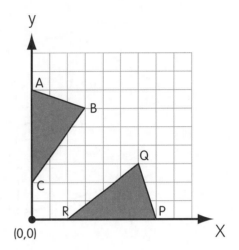

Which one is the correct description of the transformation?

- ○ rotation of 90° clockwise at (0,0) and reflection about the x-axis
- ○ translation to the right by 3 units and reflection about the y-axis
- ○ reflection in the x-axis and rotation of 180° counterclockwise at (0,0)
- ○ rotation of 90° clockwise at (0,0) and reflection about the y-axis

8 Which number is a factor of 96 and a multiple of 16?

- ○ 6
- ○ 24
- ○ 32
- ○ 64

9 Susan prepared a gift for Jack's birthday. Look at the gift box below.

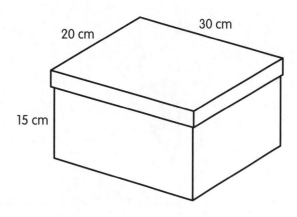

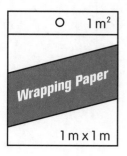

Susan has 1 m² of wrapping paper. Do you think she has enough wrapping paper to wrap the gift box? Explain.

Explain Your Thinking

10 John and Mary went strawberry picking yesterday.

John picked 2 baskets of strawberries in 10 minutes and Mary picked 3 baskets in 12 minutes.

Who picked faster?

Each basket of strawberries weighed about 4.2 kg. How many kilograms of strawberries did they pick in total in one hour?

Show Your Work

Assessment of
MATHEMATICS

Grade
6

1 Which of the following number are the sentences describing?

- It is a prime number.
- It is a factor of 52.
- It is smaller than 10.

O 2

O 11

O 13

O 21

2 Cliff drew an angle that is 90° greater than the one below.

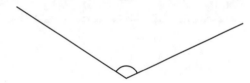

What kind of angle did he draw?

O acute

O obtuse

O straight

O reflex

3 Which pattern has this rule: "Increase by multiplying the same number to each term."?

O 4, 6, 8, 10, 12

O 6, 12, 18, 24, 30

O 7, 8, 10, 13, 17

O 2, 4, 8, 16, 32

4 A block with a square base has a side length of 21 cm and a height of 10 cm. Mr. Campbell cuts it into 2 identical parts as shown below.

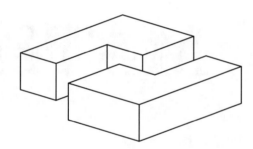

What is the volume of each part?

O 1050 cm³

O 2100 cm³

O 2205 cm³

O 4410 cm³

5 A spinner is divided into 5 equal parts and it is labelled from 1 to 5. What is the probability that the pointer will land on a prime number?

○ $\frac{1}{5}$

○ $\frac{2}{5}$

○ $\frac{3}{5}$

○ $\frac{4}{5}$

6 Which set of values is represented by the dots on the number line?

9.3   9.5

○ 9.32, 9.34, 9.36, 9.39

○ 9.32, 9.35, 9.4, 9.48

○ 9.31, 9.32, 9.41, 9.42

○ 9.33, 9.34, 9.43, 9.45

7 A triangle is drawn on the grid as shown.

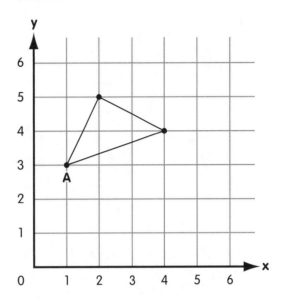

The triangle is translated 1 unit to the left and 2 units down. What are the new coordinates of point A?

○ (0,5)

○ (0,1)

○ (2,1)

○ (2,5)

8 Which number is equivalent to 5%?

○ 0.5

○ $\frac{2}{5}$

○ 0.02

○ 0.05

9 Look at the equations.

$$c + 3 = 12$$

$$c + d = 9$$

What is d?

○ 0

○ 3

○ 6

○ 9

10 Put the fractions below from greatest to least.

$$1\frac{3}{7} \quad \frac{15}{7} \quad \frac{11}{4} \quad \frac{7}{4}$$

○ $\frac{15}{7}, \frac{11}{4}, 1\frac{3}{7}, \frac{7}{4}$

○ $1\frac{3}{7}, \frac{7}{4}, \frac{11}{4}, \frac{15}{7}$

○ $\frac{11}{4}, \frac{7}{4}, 1\frac{3}{7}, \frac{15}{7}$

○ $\frac{11}{4}, \frac{15}{7}, \frac{7}{4}, 1\frac{3}{7}$

11 Mrs. Winter buys 2 cups of coffee and a bagel with cream cheese.

Menu	
Item	**Price**
Coffee	$1.45
Tea	$1.50
Sandwich	$2.85
Bagel*	$1.75

*$0.75 extra with cream cheese

What will be the change if she pays $10?

○ $4.60

○ $5.35

○ $5.40

○ $6.45

12 Which of the following is a factor of 52 and a prime number?

○ 2

○ 3

○ 4

○ 26

13 What is the missing number in the equation below?

$$36 - \square \times 3 = 60 \div 5$$

- ○ 4
- ○ 8
- ○ 32
- ○ 48

14 There are 50 guests in a dining hall. 16% of them are children. How many children are there in the dining hall?

- ○ 4
- ○ 6
- ○ 8
- ○ 16

15 A birthday cake weighs 1.2 kg. Which pair of measurements is equivalent to 1.2 kg?

- ○ 1200 mg and 120 000 g
- ○ 1200 g and 120 000 mg
- ○ 1200 g and 1 200 000 mg
- ○ 120 g and 12 000 mg

16 Look at the numbers below.

$$1\frac{2}{5} \quad 52\% \quad 1.25 \quad \frac{5}{2}$$

Put them in order from least to greatest.

- ○ $1\frac{2}{5}$, 1.25, $\frac{5}{2}$, 52%
- ○ 52%, 1.25, $1\frac{2}{5}$, $\frac{5}{2}$
- ○ 1.25, $\frac{5}{2}$, 52%, $1\frac{2}{5}$
- ○ $\frac{5}{2}$, 1.25, $1\frac{2}{5}$, 52%

17 Joe and Leslie start travelling in opposite directions from the same place. Joe is travelling at 40 km/h and Leslie is travelling at 55 km/h. How far will they be apart after 2 hours?

- ○ 30 km
- ○ 95 km
- ○ 120 km
- ○ 190 km

18 The capacities of 3 bottles of water are recorded below.

0.82 L   450 mL   0.092 L

Leo poured the 3 bottles of water into a jar that has a capacity of 2.4 L. How much more water can the jar hold?

○ 0.21 L

○ 1.038 L

○ 1.362 L

○ 1.776 L

19 What is the answer in expanded form to the number sentence below?

21.09 − 14.68 = ?

○ 6 + 0.4 + 0.001

○ 6 + 0.04 + 0.01

○ 6 + 0.4 + 0.01

○ 30 + 5 + 0.7 + 0.07

20 Jackson is making shapes with strings. He has made one square and one rectangle and recorded their perimeters and areas in the chart.

	Rectangle	Square
Area (square units)	12	9
Perimeter (units)	14	12

Which set of shapes is Jackson's?

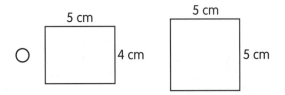

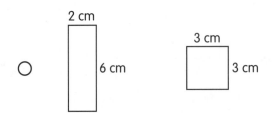

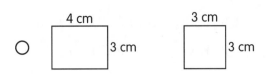

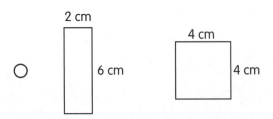

21 What are the first and the last terms in the number pattern?

_____, **7, 15, 31, 63,** _____

- ○ 3 ; 726
- ○ 3 ; 127
- ○ 4 ; 126
- ○ 5 ; 71

22 The cube below holds 0.8 kg of sand.

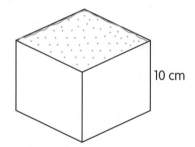

10 cm

How many kilograms of sand are needed to fill the sandbox that measures 1.2 m long, 0.5 m wide, and 0.1 m deep?

- ○ 20
- ○ 48
- ○ 60
- ○ 480

23 Which statement best describes the transformation of figure M to figure N?

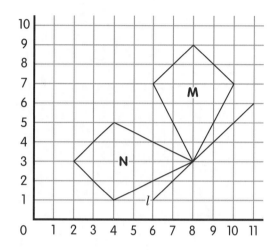

- ○ Make a $\frac{1}{4}$ turn at (3,8).

- ○ Make a $\frac{1}{4}$ counterclockwise turn at (8,3).

- ○ Reflect in line l.

- ○ Translate 6 units to the left and 6 units down.

24 0.5 L of milk makes 150 chocolate blocks. If Mrs. Collin has 2.5 L of milk, how many chocolate blocks can she make?

- ○ 30
- ○ 500
- ○ 750
- ○ 7500

25 Which of the following is a scalene triangle?

○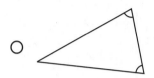

○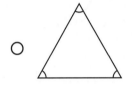

○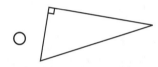

○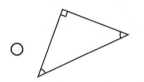

26 Laura has a collection of jewels. She uses 16 of them, which is 25% of her collection, to decorate her musical box. How many jewels are there in Laura's collection now?

○ 48

○ 36

○ 64

○ 400

27 The pictograph below shows the number of bags of chips in different flavours sold in a store yesterday.

Number of Bags of Chips in Different Flavours Sold

Ketchup	● ● ◖
Sour Cream	● ● ●
Barbecue	● ◕
Cheese	● ● ◢

● represents 8 bags.

How many bags of chips were sold in all?

○ 9.5

○ 38

○ 70

○ 76

28 Sam and George leave their warehouse at the same time to deliver the ordered items to two different places.

Sam drives at a speed of 72 km/h to City Balas and George drives at a speed of 45 km/h to Brookville.

City Balas   Warehouse   Brookville

216 km   180 km

How far will they be apart after 2 hours?

What is the difference between their arrival times?

Show Your Work

29 There was a jar of 24 chocolate eggs without peanuts. Jack took out 2 chocolate eggs from the jar and ate them.

Jack's mom puts a bag of chocolate eggs with peanuts into the jar today. The probability of drawing a chocolate egg without peanuts is $\frac{1}{3}$.

How many chocolate eggs with peanuts are there in the jar?

Explain Your Thinking

30 A wooden rectangular block is cut into two identical triangular prisms.

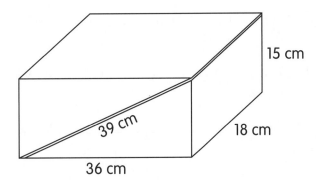

What is the volume of each triangular prism?

Mr. Campbell wants to paint the triangular prisms red. What is the total surface area to be painted?

Show Your Work

31 Bonnie drew an isosceles right-angle triangle. The length of the longest side of the triangle is 8 cm.

She cuts the triangle into 8 identical triangles. What is the area of each small triangle?

You may draw the triangle on the centimetre grid to work out your answer.

Show Your Work

32 Lori has a sticker-making machine. The number of stickers it can make depends on how much glue she has. The chart below shows their relationship.

Amount of Glue (mL)	No. of Stickers Made
2	2
4	6
6	10
8	14

If Lori puts 20.4 mL of glue into the machine, how many stickers can she make?

Lori has two bottles of glue, one 4 mL and the other 8 mL. Should she put the glue into the machine at two different times or at the same time? Explain.

Explain Your Thinking

33 There are 80 people in the school playground. 5% of them are teachers and the rest are children.

There are 60 people in the gymnasium. 0.15 of them are teachers and the rest are children.

What is the ratio of the number of teachers to all the people in each place? Which place has a higher ratio?

Show Your Work

34 The shape that Flora makes is symmetrical in line **d**.

Help her complete the shape and write the coordinates of the vertices of the shape.

Make a $\frac{1}{2}$ turn of the shape at (3,4) and write the coordinates of the vertices of the image.

Show Your Work

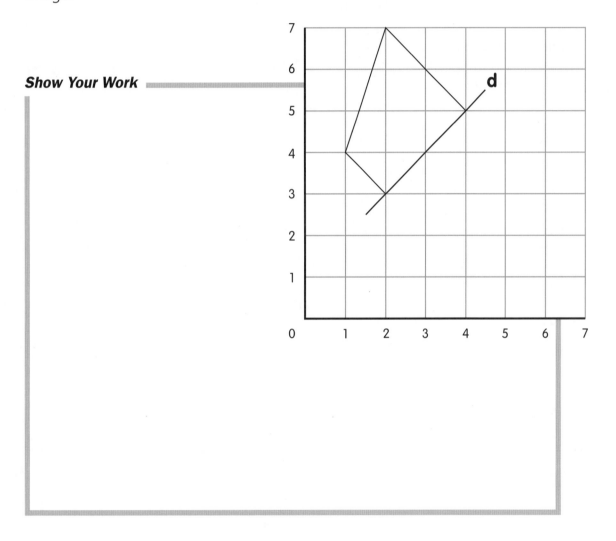

35 There is a summer sale at Eddie's Grocery Store. Every customer receives a box of orange juice for free with the purchase of 2 bags of chips.

Olivia paid $40 for 7 bags of chips at $3.86 each and some boxes of orange juice at $2 each and recieved $2.98 change.

How many boxes of juice did Olivia get in total?

Explain Your Thinking

Practice 1

1. 3
2. The maximum driving speed is 50 km in 1 h.
3. m^2
4. three quarters of a litre
5. $23   6. 22
7. $1\frac{2}{3}$, $1\frac{1}{2}$, $\frac{4}{3}$, $\frac{5}{4}$
8. Bruce has 5 more marbles than Ted.
9.
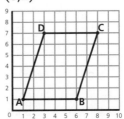
10. She buys 6 apples and 20 oranges, or 21 apples and 5 oranges.
11.
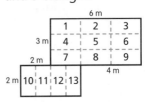
Uncle Jimmy will need 13 pieces of sod.

Practice 2

1. 2.84, 2.86, 2.90, 2.98
2. 5.617   3. 2, 3, 4, 6, 7, 8
4. 127   5. 18:08
6. 30 m^3 7. m^3
8. (8,2)
9.

It is a parallelogram. A parallelogram has 2 pairs of lines that are equal in length and parallel to each other. It also has 2 pairs of equal angles that are opposite to each other. Its area is 30 square units.
10. Mean: 53 trees ; Median: 47 trees ; Mode: 43 trees
    Janet should use the mean because it is the largest value among the three.

Practice 3

1. 18 ÷ 3   2. 41°
3. 5 cm   4. 5, 13, 21, 29, 37
5. A and C
6. 1.023, 1.203, 1.302, 1.320
7. 0.92   8. $\frac{1}{8}$

9. Time needed at normal speed: 216 ÷ 8 = 27
    It takes the robot 27 s at normal speed.
    Time needed at turbo speed: 216 ÷ 9 = 24
    Time saved: 27 – 24 = 3
    3 seconds will be saved.
10. Length of wire: (30 + 18) x 2 = 96 (cm)
    Side length of square: 96 ÷ 4 = 24 (cm)
    The side length of the square is 24 cm.
    Area of the rectangle: 540 cm^2
    Area of the square: 576 cm^2
    The square does not have the same area as the rectangle.

Practice 4

1. 480
2. B is larger than A by 3 cm^2.
3. $\frac{6}{7}$ 4. 8
5. 100 + 90 + 0.7 + 0.06
6. 19   7. 64, 32, 16, 8, 4
8. $\frac{1}{2}$ 9. B
10.
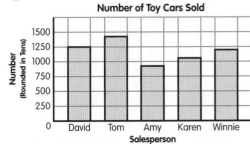
Amy's commission is closest to $600.
11. P & W: $3.96 + $2.08 = $6.04
    Onville: $4.20 + $1.29 = $5.49
    Abby should choose Onville Grocery. The total cost is $5.49.

Practice 5

1. 810   2. 9:8   3. $64
4. $2\frac{7}{10}$, 200%, 1.875
5. 265   6. 1100
7. 54   8.
9. 15
10. The probability of matching each guess:
    Guess 1: $\frac{4}{16}$; Guess 2: $\frac{6}{16}$; Guess 3: $\frac{4}{16}$
    I will choose Guess 2 because it has the greatest chance of winning a prize.

11. Tom's cards:

69

Jack's cards:

24	69 – 24 – 7 = 38	7

They share: 69 – 24 – 7 = 38 (cards)
No. of cards Tom gave Jack: 38 ÷ 2 = 19 (cards)
Tom has: 69 – 19 = 50 (cards)
Jack has: 24 + 19 = 43 (cards)
So Tom has 50 cards and Jack has 43 cards.

Practice 6

1. 1:05 p.m.
2. 2 cm
3. 550 mL
4. 0.3
5. 4
6. 6:1
7. 450 000 m
8. 1.22
9. No. of ● : 3 ; 6 ; 10 ; 15
   Pattern rule: Start at 3. Add 3 and increase the number you add by 1 each time.
   No. of balls of modelling clay with 10 layers:
   15 + 6 + 7 + 8 + 9 + 10 + 11 = 66
   Louise has 66 – 2 = 64 balls of modelling clay.

10.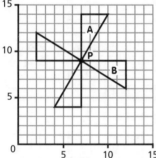

   Rotate triangle A $\frac{1}{2}$ clockwise about P and draw the image. Then rotate triangle A $\frac{1}{4}$ counterclockwise about P and draw the image.

Practice 7

1. 135° to 145°
2. $\frac{3}{8}$
3. 4 h 15 min
4. 37
5. 2810 m
6. hexagonal prism
7. (6,2)
8. 13 rows of 13 scouts
9. Left spinner: C ; Right spinner: A
   The probability that the pointer will land on red or green:
   Spinner A: $\frac{3}{8}$; Spinner C: $\frac{7}{8}$
   I will choose spinner C because the probability of winning a toy with spinner C is greater than spinner A.

10. old plot:
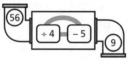
old plot: A 3 m, 2 m   new plot: B 6 m, 4 m

   Perimeter of A: 10 m ; Area of A: 6 m²
   Perimeter of B: 20 m ; Area of B: 24 m²
   Yes, the amount of fencing needed will double. The area of the new plot is 4 times the old one, so 8 bags of grass seeds are needed to cover the new plot.

Practice 8

1. It is more likely to draw red than green.
2. 130 cm/s
3. 20 cm
4. 1036
5. 178 km
6. 1.32, 1.38, 1.4, 1.45
7. 288 cm³
8. 520
9. (Suggested answers)
   input: 1 ; output: 24
   input: 2 ; output: 28
   input: 3 ; output: 32

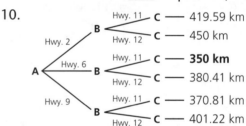

   input: 24 ; output: 1
   input: 28 ; output: 2
   input: 32 ; output: 3

10.
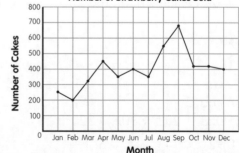

	Hwy. 11	C — 419.59 km
B	Hwy. 12	C — 450 km
B	Hwy. 11	C — **350 km**
	Hwy. 12	C — 380.41 km
B	Hwy. 11	C — 370.81 km
	Hwy. 12	C — 401.22 km

   A — Hwy. 2, Hwy. 6, Hwy. 9 to B

   The shortest route is via Hwy. 6 and Hwy. 11 through Town B. It is 350 km long.

Practice 9

1. 8
2. 16
3. 45%
4. $4\frac{5}{8}$ kg
5. 3 years old
6. 21.422 m
7. $40
8. obtuse scalene triangle
9. 25 680
10.

   Number of Strawberry Cakes Sold

   (line graph, y-axis: Number of Cakes 0–800, x-axis: Month Jan–Dec)

Average monthly sale: 400 strawberry cakes
The months that have monthly sales higher
than average are: April, August, September,
October, and November.

11.

The net forms a triangular prism which has
6 vertices, 9 edges, 2 triangular faces, and 3
rectangular faces.

Practice 10

1. $\frac{2}{5}$ 2. 1.885 L
3. 64   4. pentagon
5. 2176 cm^3 6. 151
7. trapezoid   8. 33%
9.
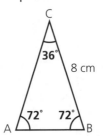

Erica's triangle is similar
to David's because the
three corresponding
angles are equal.

10. Total mark: 79 x 5 = 395
Second quiz's mark:
395 – (78 + 85 + 69 + 74) = 89
Katie got 89 marks on her second quiz.
She will need 85 x 6 – 79 x 5 = 115 (marks)
to get an average of 85, which is impossible.
So Katie will not get an average of 85 with
one more quiz.

Practice 11

1. 12   2. 200 000
3. 48, 44, 40, 36, 32   4. Each angle is 60°.
5. 36   6. $4300
7. (6,7)   8. 3:05 p.m.
9.

Area in cm^2:
A: 7
B: 12
C: 15
D: 16

He can make 4 different rectangles. The
rectangle with dimensions 4 cm by 4 cm has
the greatest area.

10.

8 cups = 1 jar   8 cups = 1 jar   1 cup = $\frac{1}{8}$ jar

Total number of jars of fruit punch drunk:

$1 + 1 + \frac{1}{8} = 2\frac{1}{8}$

They drank $2\frac{1}{8}$ jars of fruit punch in all.

Practice 12

1. 1.21   2. $\frac{5}{20}$ 3. 250 g
4. Make a $\frac{1}{2}$ turn about point K.
5. 58   6. 28
7. B   8. 2
9.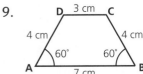

It is a trapezoid.
The perimeter of
ABCD is 18 cm, so the
wire is 18 cm long.

10. (Suggested answer)
First 4 scores in order: 53, 62, 68, 75
Choose 62 to be the median and mode, so
one of the unknowns is 62. Then find the
other unknown so that the mean is 62.
Sum of the first 5 scores: 320
Sum of all the scores: 62 x 6 = 372
Difference between the two sums: 52
So, the other unknown is 52.
The two scores are 52 and 62.

Practice 13

1. 15:20   2. 11:00 – 12:00
3. 2, 3, 2   4. 225
5. 184 cm   6. 1.2
7. 1 ; 4 ; 49   8. 2
9.

Layer	1	2	3	4	5	6	7
Side length (cm)	2	3	5	8	12	17	23
Perimeter (cm)	8	12	20	32	48	68	92

Amount of string needed for 6 layers: 1.88 m
Amount of string needed for 7 layers: 2.8 m
So, there are at most 6 layers in Jason's design.

10. No. The result is not reasonable because the
sum of the data is not 100%.
The number of children who choose
sandwich is 20% of 25, which is 5.

Practice 14

1. 34
2. 2 kg 118 g
3. 10
4. 4 h
5. 22 m²
6. 6
7. rotation of 90° clockwise at (0,0) and reflection about the x-axis
8. 32
9. Susan has 10 000 cm² of wrapping paper and she needs 2700 cm². Susan has enough wrapping paper.
10. To pick one basket of strawberries, John needed 5 min and Mary needed 4 min, so Mary picked faster.

    John picked 12 baskets and Mary picked 15 baskets in an hour. They picked a total of 27 baskets in an hour which weighed a total of about 113.4 kg.

Assessment

1. 2
2. reflex
3. 2, 4, 8, 16, 32
4. 2205 cm³
5. $\frac{3}{5}$
6. 9.32, 9.35, 9.4, 9.48
7. (0,1)
8. 0.05
9. 0
10. $\frac{11}{4}, \frac{15}{7}, \frac{7}{4}, 1\frac{3}{7}$
11. $4.60
12. 2
13. 8
14. 8
15. 1200 g and 1 200 000 mg
16. 52%, 1.25, $1\frac{2}{5}$, $\frac{5}{2}$
17. 190 km
18. 1.038 L
19. 6 + 0.4 + 0.01
20.
    ```
    4 cm            3 cm
    ┌──────┐        ┌──────┐
    │      │3 cm    │      │3 cm
    └──────┘        └──────┘
    ```
21. 3 ; 127
22. 48
23. Make a $\frac{1}{4}$ counterclockwise turn at (8,3).
24. 750
25.
26. 48
27. 76
28. Sam travelled in 2 h: 72 x 2 = 144 (km)
    George travelled in 2 h: 45 x 2 = 90 (km)
    They will be 144 + 90 = 234 (km) apart after 2 hours.

    Sam needs 3 hours and George needs 4 hours to arrive at their destinations. The difference between their arrival times is 1 hour.

29. No. of chocolate eggs without peanuts: 22
    No. of all chocolate eggs: 22 x 3 = 66
    Portion of chocolate eggs with peanuts:
    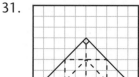
    $$1 - \frac{1}{3} = \frac{2}{3}$$
    No. of chocolate eggs with peanuts:
    $$\frac{2}{3} = \frac{44}{66}$$
    There are 44 chocolate eggs with peanuts in the jar.
30. The volume of each triangular prism is 4860 cm³. The total surface area to be painted is 4320 cm².
31.

    The area of each small triangle is 2 cm².
32. Lori can make 38 stickers with 20 mL of glue.
    4 mL makes 6 stickers and 8 mL makes 14. 12 mL makes 22 stickers. She should put the glue into the machine at the same time.
33. Ratio in playground:
    teachers: all= 4:80 = 1:20
    Ratio in gymnasium:
    teachers: all= 9:60 = 3:20
    The gymnasium has a higher ratio of teachers.
34.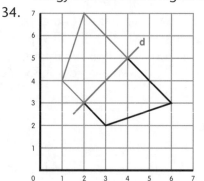

    Coordinates of the shape:
    (3,2), (1,4), (2,7), (6,3)
    Coordinates of the image:
    (3,6), (5,4), (4,1), (0,5)
35. Olivia paid $40 – $2.98 = $37.02.
    7 bags of chips cost $27.02, so Olivia spent $37.02 – $27.02 = $10 on 5 boxes of orange juice. She got 3 boxes of orange juice for free, so she has 8 boxes in total.